For Sharon,
in our meeting !

REACHING FOR LONGER WATER:

POEMS SELECTED AND NEW

David Mercier Parsons

Signature Ed. 2015

TEXAS REVIEW PRESS
HUNTSVILLE, TEXAS

W0017524

Copyright @ 2015 by David Mercier Parsons
All rights reserved
Printed in the United States of America

FIRST EDITION

Requests for permission to acknowledge material from the work should be sent to:

Permissions
Texas Review Press
English Department
Sam Houston State University
Huntsville, TX 77341-2146

Acknowledgements:

I wish to express my gratitude to the editors of the following journals and anthologies in which poems from this volume have appeared, occasionally in different versions:

Anthology of Magazine Verse & Yearbook of Poetry, Agave: A Celebration of Tequila Anthology, A Texas Garden of Verses Anthology, Beyond Forgetting: Poetry & Prose About Alzheimer's (Kent State University Press), Borderlands Texas Poetry Review, Concho River Review, Criterion, descant, Gulf Coast, Improbable Worlds: Anthology of Texas & Louisiana Poetry (Mutabilis Press), Louisiana Literature, New Texas, Numinous Magazine: Spiritual Poetry, Permian Basin Beyond 2014 Anthology, San Pedro River Review, Southwestern American Literature, Standpoints: Journal for Teachers of English in France, SWIRL: Literary & Arts Journal, The Langdon Review of the Arts, The New Review, The Texas Review, Touchstone Literary Review, The Weight of Addition: Anthology of Texas Poetry (Mutabilis Press), The World Keeps Turning To Light (Negative Capability Press), Writing Texas.

The following poems were previously published in David M. Parsons New & Selected Poems (TCU Press): "Snapping In," "Archaic Reflections on Blake's Baptism," "The Etymology of Sound," "Revenant Old Austin Songs," "The Lost Gift of Time," and "Sight, Gust of Wind."

My great appreciation to all the fine staff of Texas Review Press, especially Keely Disman, for her close reading and invaluable help with finalizing the manuscript. I am so very fortunate and humbled to have TRP's support all these many years. I also owe a special debt of gratitude to Paul Ruffin, who published three of my previous collections, greatly inspiring and gratifying me. I have been extremely fortunate to have had the gifted editorial advice and friendship of Jean Wood, Cliff Hudder, and the many colleagues, mentors, and friends—old and new—who have given me support, ideas, and memories that have been instrumental in the creation of the poems for this collection; and always, Nancy, always my 1st reader, my lover and best friend. I will also be eternally grateful to my mother, Reba Lanet Kierbow Parsons, who turned me on to reading books one lonely summer in the rolling woods of Austin, Texas.

Cover photo and cover design courtesy of Nancy Dazey Parsons, Graphic Design Group

Library of Congress Cataloging-in-Publication Data

Parsons, David M., 1943-

[Poems. Selections]

Reaching for longer water : new & selected poems 1991 - 2015 / David M. Parsons. -- Edition: first.

pages cm

ISBN 978-1-68003-032-7 (pbk. : alk. paper)

I. Title.

PS3566.A769A6 2015

811'.54--dc23

2015003441

Always
for Nancy,
Always

Contents

The Frank Gaze of Women

It's Not About Rememberiong

Color of Mourning

REACHING FOR LONGER WATER:

POEMS SELECTED AND NEW

I

AUSTIN RELATIVITY

AUSTIN RELATIVITY

The old flagship Night Hawk Restaurant sits at a memory axis—
just over the Colorado River Bridge where Riverside Drive crosses

South Congress running east toward the Bergstrom Air Force Base;
where, at the guarded entrance, the large painted water tank spouted

PEACE IS OUR PROFESSION, the home of Dr. Strangelove's
bombers of the sixties; and later, those chillingly beautiful aquiline

Phantom jets streaking over the emerald hill country rolls
in the seventies and eighties; this same road ran west past the lazy

hills of Barton Springs, where those stunningly free living hippie
sprites would play and lay topless, sprawled across the lush

north green banks…across from the icy blue pumping methodical
flow of the springs that fronted my guard stand, appearing

at times as bodies strewn like casualties of some insidious sun
bomb, as I sweltered in baby oil mixed with the bold blood

of iodine, squinting over small patches of zinc oxide, musing
to the radio sounds of the Stones, Dylan, the many varied

voices that pumped with steely laced drum beats a music
into the heart of our turbulent days, instilling an urgent urge

to physically act—to escape from the stagnant pools of our youth,
to dive into the current of whitewater energy of the times, swim

that dark and intoxicating mystery, that dangerous rushing, rushing—

NIGHT HAWK

Congress Avenue rolls south from the Paramount Theater straight
through sentries of live oak over the Colorado River before it was a lake—

over that first main bridge before it housed the dark cloud of bats
and past the flagship Night Hawk Restaurant, where, I remember

running head to chest into President Lyndon Johnson as
his secret service agents, holding the glass doors open,

looked on in horror at the unexpected possibilities
of our collision, as I swung into the double doors

like some unexpected and inescapable event in Asia,
from the snaky nook of the restroom corridor, unaware

of his incoming entourage—*s'cuse me*—*no, pardon me!*
For a brief moment we did that uncertain dance to squeeze

by each other in the small vestibule of the double door entry, LBJ
in trapped composure, I imagine, with steak or a beer on his mind—

I—in awkward and puzzled wonderment—secret service agents
on the outside and inside doors—staying stiffly cool—sizzling—

STREET FIGHTER

I remember emerging from the cool dark bowels of the Paramount Theater
into the Austin noonday summer sky—to the right was the capital building

looming over gardens of brass soldiers, fountains, and pristine walkways
guarded by old cannon; where, while working as Governor Shiver's

page, I ended lunches feeding the picket of pigeons and squirrels
high dollar Spanish peanuts from my daily visits to Lamb's Candies.

Nearer, the long gone Piccadilly Cafeteria emerges in memory on the corner,
where Tom, an old punch-drunk former Golden Gloves Champ,

sold newspapers and gave unknowingly, like some new age Christopher
Smart, his joy for life to every puzzle-faced pedestrian he could spar, his

smiling, rough and rosy square Mediterranean face with huge arthritic
hands that did not go with his compact body and the soft crazed hazel eyes

that seemed to look through you at some shadowy opponent—hawking the lives
of others with the energy and footwork of a twenty-five year old—

what is it about old warriors that hooks the enigmatic darkness camped behind,
just behind the Cain blood rim of eyes, surviving on the edges of all memories.

GREEN BEER SUMMER MORNING (1964)

The first window I smashed
was jolting—adrenalin;
shock, then euphoria—

The hard green pear looked
more the apple; lacking
the feminine lines, it fit
like a hardball in my bare
tenebrous hand, as I leaned

into that deafening blast
of south Austin air—
long lost hair stinging ruddy
adolescent cheeks, burnishing
the fleshy hunter's squint

from the back of Rusty's
white fifty-nine El Camino
as I balanced in the cocked
position for the next target
of opportunity, perhaps,

another windshield, a mailbox,
or middle class milk bottles
set neat as bowling pins
on the front door steps, or
the ideas sleeping safely
in these Barton Hills homes—

A fire was in our heads—
a force that wanted to consume
anything neatly wrought—everything
that held with institutional form,
the empty promises—we sensed
a mirroring vulnerability—we rifled

the young summer morning air
of Austin with the detached
green hardness of youth, we
were the fire, the fire
of that other green fuse—
we without knowing, were a part
of the dark new American morning.

SHIRTS VS SKINS

South of the Night Hawk, Congress Avenue begins a slow rise
past the Texas School for the Deaf with its institutionally

correct buildings standing stoically affront the street
hiding the rough-hewn athletic field behind; where,

a handful of us would gather for the weekly Sunday afternoon
rituals, those "All American" pick-up tackle football games—

shirts vs. skins—we would perform diving tackles—crashing
rolls—braving those clandestine goat-headed stickers grown

like small land mines into the deceptively green lushness
of the spear grass laced field, trying on that eternally inbred

concept of man: this uniquely dark and gloriously dumb mantle
of our species: giving up our bodies to some high, brotherly cause—

THE RAPIDS

From above, Barton Springs appears in widening blue, a landing strip,
a destination of water at right angles to the river that was pooled
into Town Lake and only a mile from my boyhood home in Rollingwood,

just a short bike ride that was mostly downhill—made shorter in time
if you knew the small rough worn and rocky back trail that ran along
Barton Creek's wooded shoreline—a blurring tangle of cedar, wild vines,

scrub oak, pecan trees, all holding watch over the whispers of sundry lovers
and the gleeful errant boys swimming the rapids toward Campbell's Hole
(we called it Camel's Hole), boys pretending their small lives wild and large

braving leeches, snapping turtles, water moccasins, and imaginary Indians,
as they would make their willowy bodies into human torpedoes shooting
the rapids—the ancient limestone tubular creek bed—arms extended forward

and hands and heart open to the flood of possibilities—any unseen jut of boulder
that might be ahead—the roiling, foaming water taking briefly, complete control
of their lives—the rushing, gushing rides—like destiny itself—dispatching them

turbulently to some rock solid and unforeseen future that might alter forever
their lives—rushing, rushing white water, a bubbling blindness that numbed
with cold—thrilled with anticipation, the delicious arbitrariness, the purest form

of the dark pleasure of risk, of the ineffable nature of the joy of giving one's body up—

AUSTIN FIRE

Memories from the day of the University of Texas Tower shootings & the 100th anniversary of Sholz's Beer Garden on August 1, 1966.

Out of the cave
of European History class
I am struck
by squinting bright skies
strolling on the edge of the shadow
of the university tower shade
through the southeast campus quad
flip-flopping to my Mustang
for my short drive to work
less than an hour before
student victim #1
will have fallen
in that very path.

I am traveling back now—
back to the pool—
down the hot tar entry
down the pebbled walkway
to Barton Springs
churning shadowy deep blue—
it's the blues—the gushing
blues 68 degrees year-round
offering a deadening numbness
making the youngest of skin
cadaver cold and this ordinary
workday, I am just another Life-
guard cut loose too soon.

And now—again
I am driving back
again back and away
away from the many
oblique precipices—falls

hidden undercurrents
jutting stones in the blinds
of the limestone aquifer
traveling back under and through
the towering pecan trees
just a short dash—and now again
Barton Springs Road—
The Rolling Stones—*Can't Get No
Satisfaction*…everything
is heating up the day.

At Sholz's Garden
another grand spring
100 years of beer flowing
unjudgmentally through
the many unruly seasons
through the untold
joyous and unfettered
the anonymous generations
of the deemed and the damned
and all their wagging
Did you know(s)…flying
around the ever blank
pages of air—air that receives, never
recording a single loving or gnashing word
of the produce of this imperfect garden
those sweaty hound dog days—I feel
that very air here again now—the gamey
smells of the Dutchman's beer garden
the carefree summer women
laughing braless in loose tie-dyes
swilling nickel Lone Stars
aiming flirtatious glances
then firing their deadly frank stares
swinging suntanned legs
to the juke box beats
*Hey, Mr. Tambourine Man
play a song for me*…all
positioned between

the two towers: the capitol dome
topped with Lady Liberty
and UT's apex and bastilles of education
and there now…and again—white puffs—

Sniper! Sniper!

Girls first! diving under
stone gray concrete tables
towering turquoise sky
ragged clouds
ripping the battle blue
drifting…mist like…hiding
momentarily gun site portals,
and our shade tree bunkers
fiery memories
imbedded
like so many stray shots—

He was a crew cut
every mother's son
Boy Scout—Marine
sharpshooter
again all paths of mine—
In his last note to the world
Charles Whitman
requested an autopsy
with special consideration
to his brain…they found
a tiny, cloudy gray mass
of malignant tissue lined
in crimson—seems it's
always the smallest of embers.

THE PRIDE

for Jeff Jamar, Terry Banard, Rusty Wier,
Bubba Johnson, Robert Leffingwell, and Steve Thompson

Running with those young lions so many years ago offers up
memories of each that are ineffable…their individual aspects
are wound around in me—timbres of song—ruddy Swede; tough
as a fence post, mythic storyteller Terry's infectious laugh; Steve
with his strutting bravado and his Flip Wilson smile; lumbering
Robert, a Saint Bernard in another life; and brilliant Jeffery John's
tall and angular Cherokee presence—I cannot pen in a single line
the unique aspects each imbued in a single line—each deserves an entire poem,
odes that when chased, escape into random memories—fragments, like

those countless Austin summer evenings, we would all cram inside and out
of our group troubadour Rusty Wier's El Camino (he named Tom)…it was our
weekend ritual of cruising like sharks from the Holiday House on Barton Springs
Road south to the Pig Stand, across from the Texas Theater on South Congress
to peruse each hang-out for whatever was happening…always on the prowl
for a carnal teasing glance—a fresh glowing new face—blond pigtail—laughing
into a coke and fries, or the other testosterone rush of some rival's challenge
framed in a car window glare—as we would glide by—their orbiting tail fins
crouched in chrome—glaring red—a ritual that has become an American pop
culture cliché and though we long for that animal quiver that always triggers
the nostalgic images so intricately meshed in memory with those pyrotechnic
sounds: Buddy Holly, Elvis, The Stones, The Beatles, The Eagles, The Beach Boys,
Simon, Garfunkel, Peter, Paul & Mary, Motown—the list just keeps humming—

We can't deny the outrage of it all: the Pollyanna idealism that took us, in less than
a score of rockin' years, from what seemed to be the hard earned clarity of a proud
Ozzie & Harriet society to blurring interventions—changes that questioned all
that seemed settled by the mid-fifties; changes that even brought into question
the validity of all questions—there is in Africa an exotic Magicicada species
that transforms itself every seventeen years—the number of years seems odd

and a bit arbitrary—their tymbals bringing forth a unique and wild new song, music that on a long summer night, is said to fill the trees; and after one listens for a while, these sounds, resonating in a single chant, singing the haunting voice of the sacred.

TWO DOGS HOWLING AT THE MOON

for Rusty Wier

I will always remember the last time I saw you,
at your *Angel's*, Tricia's crowded Plano townhouse

and how, after our four hours of harmoniously
catching-up on thirty some odd years of lost time,

I read you my poem *The Pride*, about that pack
we ran with—we thought we were lions, we were

more wolves or stray dogs—reliving those old stories
of growing up together wild in the enigmatic sixties

in South Austin, like our Tequila drinking contest
when I came home from the Marines, how I passed

out hearing you strumming to *Rave On*, learning
later, you had quickly followed me to the darkness

falling dead-drunk onto your beat up old guitar,
like some faithful warrior falling on his sword.

As our visiting ebbed, you played for me the second
of your three new songs, saying, *"I'm still writing—*

can't stop doing that one thing—we're like those two
old dogs in my song, David, we writers just keep barking

and howling at that ole' moon," your voice still
inimitably valved despite the chemo and the thousands

of songs poured out like manna to the many hungering
audiences of the nightlife you so loved and I remember

at that moment thinking how Li Po is said to have so
adored that great luminous orb that he perished, when

after a night of heavy drinking, he fell into the lake
attempting to embrace the dazzling antediluvian body, tumbling

head-long and alone into the deep ink of oblivion,
or perhaps, the masked reflections of an eternal light

and how you, after sailing through countless gigs
and seas of Agave, one complimentary shot at a time,

were now arduously floundering to make the best of each
of these last painfully clumsy egregious moments,

like you always have, with that distinctive dancing
twinkle in the weathered squint of those smiling blue

eyes, eyes still fully alive in my memory, still dancing—

I suppose every human passion holds within its core
the germ of something lethal to its being and yet,

somehow, interwoven with the potential of rapture.
Tonight the sheer linen curtains of my bedroom seem

to be tossed by the blurring energy of the moonlight
bouncing glowing stones across the dark water of our pool

as the ceiling fan circles in its perpetual waving orbits
and I can hear my daughter's tiny lap dog underneath

my small dinghy of a bed gnawing like memories
on a T-bone scrap from dinner, he is at that phase

where all the meat is flayed away and one can only
hear the sound of bone against bone as he is working

into a rhythm in his ceaseless mastication, creating
his own unique kind of wild, raw and satisfying music.

REVENANT OLD AUSTIN SONGS

I.

When Chubby Checker's voice emerges again
resurrected from my oldies radio station
with that iconic first line invitation,
    Come on baby, let's do the Twist…,

it is again as the first time I heard it, and there
       within are Jane Wolf and Kay Goodnight petitely
    Twisting, Twisting, Twisting
         taut teen bodies,

blond ponytails bouncing with the stirring beat,
at the Hancock Recreation Center's Teen Night, back
in a hot and gamey room crowded with gawking
adolescents seeing the latest dance for the first time,

having no idea that this moment was one of a beginning
of an era when the term, *blow your mind*, was the norm,
all jammed into one of the small rooms in my head, among
the many memories of those summer early sixties evenings.

II

When The New Christi Minstrels chime in velvet voices
so perfectly feathered together from my old 78 LP,
    Today, while the blossom still clings to the vine,
*I'll taste your strawberries; I'll drink your sweet wine…*there

is Patty's moon face floating timelessly below mine: flush
cheeks of pearl, our youthful sinewy limbs all akimbo, pungent
tang of college girl hormones—*I will feast at your table, I'll sleep*
in your clover who cares what tomorrow shall bring….

another relationship like so many, many poems,
long published, and yet, for years, wrongly compiled, surfacing
in flashes, surprising jolts of emotion and regret, a raw chord
emerging off-key from memory's chthonic jaded catacombs.

III

When Carol King moans in her *Tapestry*, *So far away*,
why can't people stay in one place anymore?—I'm clinging
in stuttering rhythms again to ideal love—inimitable Terry,
our Austin stone split-level home hanging perilously

like a naive rock climber to the hillside of Walnut Creek,
the azure of the dark water swimming pool, suspended
like a dense watery cloud, sky on sky above hill country
live oaks, cedars, wild vines and scrub brush clinging

precariously to the crags below our bedroom window,
Bran-Cook's five-year-old feet doing that nightly dance
around the deep sunken pit of our airy vaulted living room
to our ardent young marriage bed, her childhood night

time fears, so vividly realized in me now, her small pads
of feet, like some masterful sound technician bringing
that unlikely mix of nostalgic joy and regret, impossible
to safely separate, like the slime of some rare, splendid fish.

INTEGRATION 1964

When James Brown's band
or most any Motown Group,
hits one of those ecstatically high
shrilling passionate sax notes, sweaty
Phil, tie loose, is swimming *The Gator*
on the gritty dance floor at Charlie's
Playhouse in after-hours' deep East Austin,
when it was the "bad part of town"
and we were like giddy young tourists
and I can taste wee-hour fried chicken
from nearby Ernie's Chicken Shack
and recall how we were always too high
to worry about the rumor of sleepy cooks
spitting into our honky customers' gravy
& mashed potatoes, we were flying our lives
through the sixties and we didn't have a clue
that we were like the Ugly Americans.

KNUCKLE BALL

We were a true blue baseball family.
Not that we didn't care for football or basketball,
we loved all the sports. The ritual begun by
our traveling salesman father, a former pitcher,
we would listen to the Yankees and Dodgers
on the radio—he loved Pee Wee Reese—and then
he would hit us ground balls in the front yard
on those slow hot Austin weekend days, the rare times
he was home from pitching Higgins Slacks on the road.

It was the only activity, I can recall, we did solely
with him—the single thing he would happily do
with us without a strong urging from our mother.
My brother Donnie was the best…glove hand magic
in retrieving the worm burners Dad would hit at us
from across the sidewalk that cut the yard in half
and often would give the ball an extra little hop
to be dealt with, as we would try to go to one knee
blocking positions, as he always coached us to do,
to make sure that if our hands were too slow or
we faltered in our judgments, our bodies would
make the stop—take the blow—thus saving a hit
to the neighbor's driveway or worse, the street
taking the ball down the steep incline of the hill
to the wild surrounding thick cedar country woods.

Our father never showed overt partiality to Donnie,
however, his body language and his hazel eyes gleamed
the pride in my brother's innate skills and though I think
our youngest brother Jerry was too young to perceive it,
I remember feeling a twinge in my chest, in the vicinity
of the heart, a painful plunk of envy, like one of those bad
hops—my father, he could throw a perfect knuckleball,
a deceptive pitch that comes at you surprisingly slow, vibrating
weirdly, creating an illusion of the ball's true path—true purpose—
I could hit his knuckleball—his best pitch—better than anyone.

AUSTIN CHILD

for Brandy

I did not call you again tonight.
Again tonight, like so many times

since I have been gone from your nights,
I thought of you as you were years ago

on that last April evening,
your blondness sleeping curled

around cordless air in a small hug of self.

I had hunted softly your bed
by the window, above Walnut Creek.

On bedroom carpet-knees bending,
hostage hands behind me, I trailed

the gamey smell of five-year-old
to breaths as a fluttering moth—

mirroring beats, mirroring beats—

finding you without touching you,
missing you two weeks at a time,

all part of a strange ritual of measured
loving, in which, we monks of infinite

resignation lay awake without calling
while my child in Austin sleeps—

sweat of sleep humidifying my mind.

AUSTIN CHILD 2005

for Dr. Brandy Cook Parsons-Miller

I am thinking of my Austin Child, Bran-Cook
she is a study in persistence, moving, always moving
with a unique ease, that familiar graceful way through
the many gates that guard the entrances to her dreams.

I am thinking of my Austin Child in Dallas, where
she has passed through one of the last passageways
that challenged her entry to the community of healers—
souls that cultivate the gray and grounded—anguished minds.

I am remembering the many days in the vast untended garden
of memories that have brought her to this day—June 3, 2005
the colors and hues: dark winter doubts, joyous blooming springs—
a journey breathed in the always present bouquet of laughter—

humor that she shared and has always been found in the darkest
of corners of our own lived days, those clock watched hours
we each—in the community of men and women—the bastille
of family—all face when cornered in thought—lone castaways

on barren islands—I am thinking today of my Austin Child—
it is tomorrow—next year—many years and thoughts from now—
she is carefully trimming fresh cut wild flowers for a cherished vase
the way she has learned to garden an individual mind, delicately

arranging the oblique and discursive thoughts to allow for a calming
blossom—the centering eye, planting verdant bulbs—fusing new views
for a few minutes, maybe a day, a week, another year, a transformed life,
bringing a small portion of a forgotten joy, lost treasure back into the lives

of the many brothers and sisters of the grand arboretum.

LIFEGUARD

We can agree to the memories
of brutalizing fireflies
in our own unique and sinister
ways. And the smell of chlorine
on the dry chafed skin is the same
in the summer saunas that were
my Austin and your St. Louis.
You have your long vacation days
in your pedophile neighbor's guard-less
pool, blurred in your memory,
like peering through a panic-fogged mask,
after being held down under the water,
under the years—reminds me
of my endless longing for someone
to save on the many sleepy days
of Lifeguarding Barton Springs,
those deep, cold, clear waters
that brought me the hot hippie girl
swimmers tugging at my draw string
mind with their long well-kempt bodies, breast
and buns aching sun, shortening
the hours of light and cool

evening baseball games at Disch Field;
and ice cold watermelon stands,
with a touch of salt for the tongue,
as bare, tanned damp legs dance
that lusty music-less tune under
the green picnic tables on the hard
dry dirt floor; or the evening, Rusty and I
hid Lone Star beer and Juicy Fruit gum
in a Scarbrough's shopping bag,
and giggled like girls into the Paramount
Theater balcony to watch some long forgotten
screaming horror movie, only
to get kicked out by an usher, when
an empty bottle got away—rolling

down the concrete stair steps,
each step
sounding
an agonizing
report of loss.

Gone are those lost moments
at the Big Chief Drive-In, watching
Doris Day fantasies while squirming
around on the sweaty vinyl seat covers,
contorting within the shelter
of our one man-made fog
around the transmission hump,
the snare of pedals, strange
zippers, buckles, clips, and the damn
gear shift knob—

Buddy Holly was sweet in the air
of almost everything in between.
All summer fire and glorious
memories to me until
I think of you and those cruel dark
voids of yours, the blurry depraved
pool, that private swimming hole
without a guard,
that you must dive back into, time
and time again, but now, know
you are not alone.

HOME

Dante was banished from his hometown
and spent a lifetime of ink an itinerant—never
being allowed to return—except after

he was dead and his bones were so very famous
that the city fathers of Florence stole
what was left of him—entombing the framework

of the man—absent flesh and the blood
that was only a couplet of his essence that had pined
for the old digs—Bob Dylan has said

his entire life of songs had been a journey back
to some anonymous home that was
for him unattainable as he had never accepted

the stretch of iron land that was his youth
as anything but coincidental and strangely alien to his
nature—nature, where, I suppose those

such as, Emerson, Thoreau, Whitman, and maybe now
Annie Dillard someday holds the promise of a home....
No doubt, their bones would all fancy the grass

as the great American bard said, *becoming the uncut beards*
of their graves and be content to trade
the blood of meat for Thomas's green fuse—my father found

himself home in a veteran's cemetery in Houston
my mother remains in a small box waiting to be returned
anywhere but Georgia red clay of her birth, or

with my father. I have been trying, if only in my mind
to return home to a lush Austin memory
planted deep—back to that violet crown of cedar, pecan,

live oaks and the lake bled hill country that from the air
appears as sleepy morning lovers a tumble under some grand
fecund blanket, back to my native soil, back

to those early roots reclaiming that ground for a sweet
while, before my brother spreads me, as I have
often directed, over the constant cold waters of Barton Springs

in the pitch of a burnished Texas evening to swirl
for a paean while in the sublime before I settle as more
grist for my primordial limestone tomb.

II

FIRE: ART & LITERATURE

FIRE

After Jo, La Belle Irlandaise (Johanna Hifferman)
by Gustave Courbet

At first glance, Johanna Hifferman appears
to be brushing her stunning long red hair,
hair filling the frame as it forms her looming
intense face, where dazzling blue eyes blaze
into a hand held silver mirror, as the other
hand toils at fiery ringlets, petite fingers pulling
gently from atop the creamy painting of brow
above the magnetic passion of those eyes,
eyes drawing the looks of the crowded queue
all gawking like the awed bystanders watching
some grand building aflame, their attention
keeps returning to the two small windows, where
humanity might emerge, showing its true
face, some emotion, like fear, despair, desire,
lust, emotions they might all recognize within
themselves or their outed longings, all standing
like worshippers before some magnificent
cardinaled saint, like Joan herself, burning,
flaming…inside and out…all present—blessed
with fire.

FEATHERING DEEP

After Edward Hirsch's
"The Angel and the Demon"

I believe it to be
unlike any other
conveyance

the manner in which
it carries us in
upon its own silence

the way an idea drifts
into the grey divide
where we find ourselves

in that sacred state—easing
quietly into the dark *duende*
to unconscious understanding

a lone canoe at midnight—blades
paddling deep—smoothly
and deftly feathering

that largest of bodies

GUST OF WIND

A landscape painting by Courbet

Could this be Eden after the fall?
The great oak tree vacant of life,
living waters abandoned, mirroring

the dark blue mood of an angry God,
zealous sky flourished with the effects
of His last enraged pronouncement

a swirling black caped cerulean composition
casting His shadow over the small bit of light
that lingers, holding the remnant warmth

in the rocks that once gave them rest?
The sky is an aspect of an ocean, where
death commingles with life and even

castaway fruit is soon absorbed, adding
to that uniquely tart, fecund fragrance
of the inland sea's gusty birthing breath

of the many bold bodies destined to come.

EVENING AFTER EATING RAINBOWS
(CAUGHT ON MYSTIC LAKE)

A partially found poem—for the Van & Kathryn Wood family

Bohumil Hrabal wrote that every beloved object
    is the center
of a garden paradise
    and everything that lives
must have its mortal enemy—
Lao-tze said that to be born
    is to exit, to die is to enter—
Rimbaud wrote that the battle of spirit
    is as terrible as any armed conflict
and Kierkegaard said you cannot separate
    the slimy from the golden fish
(without killing the fish)—
    in a polluted river running
through stretches of factories
    a beautiful fish may sometimes
be found sparkling like an eye—

Once a man collected books on aviation
    because he thought Icarus
was Jesus' forerunner—
    are we all like olives: only
when we are crushed
    do we yield what is truly
the best in us—
Inquisitors burn books in vain—if a book
    has anything to say, it burns
with a quiet laugh, because
    any book worth its salt points
up and out of itself—

When we were young lovers
    so transfixed
with the complexities, especially
    of the sensual body

we had to say everything
    with our hands
In the starry firmament of night
    the senses lie dormant,
an immortal spirit speaks
    in a nameless tongue
of things that may be grasped
    but not described

After an evening considering all these found
    thoughts in your small body of fire,
I could easily coil inside myself
    like a cat in winter
but it is midnight and I am back
    on the outskirts of Absarokee, named
for the Crow, looking directly above,
    into the ebony wings of an unambiguous
Montana sky, my head arched up—
    and out—spinning—spinning—
in *Too Loud a Solitude*—

SOUND HEARD ONLY
AT POETRY READINGS

Because of the church like atmosphere of most readings
any sound made is first perceived as rude intrusion, not
this sound, which could be someone clearing their throat
but for the few of the audience that chime in guttural unisons

Uumm

It could be the reaction of someone asked to choose
their favorite Emily Dickinson or Walt Whitman
poem to read before a crowd of accomplished poets
and scholars Pub-full of the spirits of Walt, of Emily

Or perhaps only the assessment made by a thoughtful
person in making most any difficult decision like
which dessert to choose from a really fancy tray
of treats: Chocolate Moose, Cheese Cake, Crème Brûlée,

Chocolate…yes, yes, it is like chocolate or pancakes
or perhaps, the compliments of a new friend or suitor
in that the number of times it is actually heard may
somehow, begin to negate its value to the palate

Or the same utterance made by lovers at the beginning
ecstasies of their pyrotechnic first touch and mindful
awareness, the oblique sensations of sexual contact.
Yes, it is that first discovery of a rare entity—a taste of a body

Uumm

STILL LIFE

It is the day after
your seventy-ninth birthday
and I have been reading poems
by Billy Collins—the one
to the invisible reader
prefaced with the Yeats
epigram: *a poet…never*
speaks directly, as to someone
at the breakfast table—
perhaps, this has been the problem,

my many failed direct attempts
to write about you, to you, celebrate
or bemoan you, that Georgia
red clay realist you…cast
in grand lifelong romantic fervor.

Nancy has been painting a still life
all week, fixing an eggplant's
bold bruise to the blood of merlot
spilled into a single glass stem
beside three green apples.
I have been unable to pick
the specific fruits or wines
from your life-filled bounty
to place carefully on a page
where, the swell of the color
of a moment like my first
awareness of your intense individuality
might be reflected subtly on to egg-
plant skin of my skin—blood
of my blood.

WOLF ATTACK

Western Art in a Cloudcroft Cafe

The eye first finds
a cowboy turning
'round—the pace, loose
couplets of thought wolves,
not the deep sounding
of the whirling snowy
storm in the ominous dark
stand of twisted evergreens
nor the spooked
palomino held
so tense between
halter and the white
grip of the rider's
hand—the swirling
becomes the focus
on the strands, where
the bulging eye
of the noble beast
in dumb eloquence
articulates all—
the all we share
framed in the vortex
of our inner weather, our
own unique ambushes,
the confined chaos, a circling
trail of claw prints
we cage within—all
the things in our head
left unsaid—

READING "OLD HEART"

for Stan Plumly

I have been diving
into your heart
for weeks now
like some lone bear
returning to a kill
not always directly—

meandering through
your *Meandering* through
trees that are rivers—branches,
alive with Magpies and Blue Jays,
many, many Jays, and Spirit Birds
taking me to more water, streaming

rivulets that run like blood, life's
milk from the many varied sources,
observations of the natural world, blood
being always present, inescapable
while feeding, head and heart,
rib deep in that divine carcass

of your mind's eye, bloody
run off from all our carnivore
hearts is everywhere I look—
I know, I know there are butterflies,
flowers, an abundance of flora,
the heart-felt human conditions,

and I should be feeling Keatsian
and I do, but I can't help thinking, too
of that massive tome: Ted Hughes.

BLINDS

After John Grave's "Goodbye to a River"

I have languished
in the chill
of a deer stand
at dawn in wait—
watching for those
jeweled eyes

to wander through brush-
land trees—sleek auburn
presences lithely moving
through the dawning
air, rich with the hot
stink of life, as

I huddled damp
in the steam of my
own heat, the bluing
cold of my rifling
dark on dark—in
the swirling shadows
of the last fading

of evening's many
deaths, slayings that
went without a report
I could discern
in my blind of artificial
trees, and yet, I
am, also, a witness

and citizen of the ancient
tribe, that coalition
that exist in the universal
chain of fear

and food—the aiming
eyes behind our many
individual stands—

all narrowing our sights,
those many faceted irises,
eyes we see through—
not with.

RE-RESURRECTION

When you began the series of endangered species posters
I could think only of that yellow bore of *National Geographic*,
its four-colors bleeding periodically to death, taking thoughts down
that endless earth line that always returns to where it began.

The old cookie canister tin between your legs that held the fuses
of color, stayed crotch-hot as I laughed at the irony
of animal crackers parading around the volley, as
if in celebration of your passion, unaware we had
eaten their bread-brothers, biting their heads off first.
An Arctic Fox in snowy-eyed wonderment
followed a Prairie Chicken's
moldy-orange strut
through the gray
tumbles.

Then
after you'd penciled
that ridiculous Brown Pelican proud,
that the Eagle came—

re-resurrecting
the thoughts of them—
fellow Marines
I could not live without
sixteen years
dead.

AMONG RENOIR FACES

Moving through the litany of those fully realized faces,
cheeks of wine flushed—conserved—confined within
the frames of their own corporeal moments, I found
a likeness—something almost family in their making,
fuzzy, supple and if not jovial, on the cusp of laughter
then Tilla, Tilla Dureiux's eyes met mine in the crowd
of the queue and I am transported to 1914 Berlin—
the day before her day-view performance in Shaw's play,
she is sitting so stately in that Paul Poiret gown for the master
yes, yes, I remember you—that captured very essence of you
on display with all the others in the Kimbell Art Museum—
Tilla Durieux in *pre-Pygmalion* grace that stopped the queue
of admirers, as the memory of *mein Liebchen* stops me now,
in a deeper state of glandular awe of her revenant life force,
the windless whisper of cerulean blue eyes set in the pale
palettes of those high cheekbones with the slight crush of red
berries beneath the delicate skin of a young snow—eyes
like no others, yet, akin to lover's eyes witnessed in every century
transfixed on their quarry—teetering intensely on the quay—
at that transcending moment when that grandest of passions
is fully realized, blind as a painted portrait, yet, peering directly
through me to something astonishing, something eternal—

CHURCH GOING OPEN SESTINA 2010

I am thinking about Phillip Larkin's uniquely masterfully
penned poem, *Church Going*, a chillingly cynical musing
about churches and what they may become when all faith
has left us all to the hard, hard wiring of the coming Tech age.
I am in the third row of St. Joseph quaint old Catholic Church
in Fort Stockton, Texas and Father Manimala's compelling voice

sounding of India, flows sublimely over the flock, rapt in his voice
and witnessing the total acceptance of this diminutive Asian's masterful
celebration of the Eucharist in a mostly Latin American church
dotted with us few white faces I am struck with my own musings
about the viability of the universal global message in our exigent age.
Will these small communities, braced with a few foreigner's faith

endure the onslaught of the discursive information age, where faith
in anything unseen has become superstition? The stark reason of voices
of reason is what remains, leaving wanting the grown-up children of our age
to wander back into these old sanctuaries with that subtle hunger for a Master
to rekindle in their being the mysterious assurances of the inward musings
that might help clarify their lives. Behind and above, the choir fills the church

with *God Bless America*, as it is the 4th of July and the small church
is similar to all Catholic Churches in our country, the icons of a faith
in all the usual places: a large crucifix with Christ's last pain, musings
hung on a large mural of blue sky, a stand of pines giving subtle voice
to community inclusion, alabaster family table, Lamb relief: Master
carrying the flag of peace besides the matching A+Ω lectern: ageless

symbols in the timeless atmosphere stoked by the past seekers for our age.
So Phillip, I think, yes, just as you said it *pleased* you to stand in the church
of your poem, the many souls born since you posed your querying masterpiece
and the unborn to follow, will keep coming, seeking some sort of fruitful faith
to quell the raw hunger that you also perceived in us and so eloquently voiced
those many years ago; and as I recall the tone of your words again, the musings

are tinged with the slightest bit of a wonder, perhaps, a passing curious musing of what it would be like to have allowed yourself an opening even at your age to the possibility of the impossible, to have entertained the intimate inner voice that has whispered to the wisest of men, bringing them dazed to some church, as you said, to *a serious house on serious earth*, where green groundless faith may be discovered, nurtured, blossoming within, filling the dull void, mastering

the mindful muse that must reason, icy analytical thinking, finding no true church, only aged *frowsty barns* for storing the hewn imaginings of those few faithful, yet, that querying murmur remains: *in death, might we be the master?*

FROST CRITICS

There are those who see
    an old snake losing
        an early skin

or some grand tree grown
    beyond its root
        connection

to the verdant earth—bark
    sailing away
        as pages torn

from some tall, proud
    story. And planted,
        solidly set

against the crush
    of New England green,
        the frozen

reds of fall—Panistic
    dreams—but this life holds
        both ground and sky—

bold among scrub
    brush and lesser
        trees. This birch reaches

and bends for both:
    young boys and ancient
        wind—this flaking,

immortal
    with
        endless skin.

"PORTENTS OF INSCAPE"

Phrase found in Ange Mlinko's review in Poetry

Someone once said you must kill a poem to dissect it,

yet, I find blades of life here: the word, *portent*,
may be an indication that something unpleasant
is about to happen, perhaps, a personal prophecy,

omen or a wonderful and marvelous thing—destiny?

and inscape: the distinctive and essential
inner quality of something, especially
a natural object or scene in nature

like the manner in which a poem resides

curled within the intricate intertwining
of the yin and yang of the many writers
so fecund of all the enigmatic possibilities

for something new, fruitful,
an entity
lit from within.

THE BACK ALLEY RABBIT OF MAIDA VALE

At first glance a cat-black sphinx—
city-stiff and stoical—living
on the rooftop stoop
with a pigeon's
back-life view
and all those angular
moons set round.

Grey fantasies of winter
fires forming forest, thick
and rising to ashen skies, offering
ghostly holograms
for the flat shingled down.

Not unlike our own dreams, timeless
moments of another time,
where wild cabbages and corn grass
flourish, then disappear in the clouds
of brook and floating breezes
of loping deer. And buried, buried
deep in the heart-beat
of years, is that other fire,
and always close by
in the tumbles, slight flashes
of yet another gray and chill

and trimming black of fox.

FALLING

After a laboring climb up the fifty finely honed granite
steps entering the Blanton Museum's beginnings, I find you

falling to the robed rock, as if you might have just kicked
a goal or been pushed roughly down by playful schoolmates.

Perhaps, you are taking a short breather before rising again
to the playing field to exact a young man's prankish revenge,

your four limbs though, somehow erecting the vacant air—
left short, accentuating the missing hands…missing feet—

your face with that innocent youthfully blank expression,
like the game face of players of all the serious contests of man.

The nameplate above identifies the body, yet, inconclusively
as *Dionysus or Heracles* and states, you are a copy, expendable

in a way…merely a casting from the ruins of Parthenon's Circle
of Pheidias, yet, in finding you here in Austin on this unhistoric

sweltering morning of June 2008, I am wishing for a place to fall, sit
and recover, not from the climb—from the single chilling inescapable

thought—you are neither the god of wine missing a wistful hand
holding forth a marbled cup of the vine, nor the son of Zeus—today

I am reminded of agonizing images on the news from Walter Reed Hospital,
our own young Marines and Soldiers falling back home to us—not unlike

warriors of every century through the many stair stepping years of history—
we always think of time as progress, moving up toward the lofty air of gods,

yet, here, this moment, I find myself witness again to a player such as you—
cast as a casualty of civilizations latest stumble—after all these centuries,

we are still falling—

WHITMAN

Is this a night hawk
trapped in the squinting light
of a clear, blue
admonishing sky,
like a ragged, dusky cloud?

Or a spotted hawk caught
shadowing inland over deeper
blue beginnings—yearnings
with the circular moaning
the slight incisions wings
must make in the wind
in order to fly.

Did this focus of feather streak, beaking
sunward, toward that seething presence
of all color before its dive
to fathoms—the timelessness
that scatter deft-white
feathery tongues.

into a multitude of mouths
singing mellifluous songs—celebrations
of a father seas's passion
for the harboring breast
of a thousand naked beaches
and a thousand more
cloaked shores—destinations
eventually found by us all
with or without
the searching.

THUMBNAIL I: ELIOT

The ledger is not a journal
but rather a collection
of anonymous deaths.
Trees, processed
to colorless
remnants,
pressed
to stiff plots
of board.
Midwestern cow; tanned
and dyed,
the color of old blood.

Inside, the neat columns:
discursive
anguish
of another multitude—
carbon stealing white

flailing of pages,
each
bordered precisely;
tracked
by one thin vein-
like line, where
each

is tethered—
a link to clarity,
sinews of ink
linking
the common,
the commonality
of a time.

THUMBNAIL II: POUND

Out of the cold pallor
of a dead face, a dark
army
of exclamations
still grows.
The beard
is not unlike
a royal robe,
a London cloak,
or rain—
the splashed shrouds found
in the slow processions
toward ultimate
truths—
dotted with the occasional
gray of half-wrongs—
still
boldly pointing…pointing—

THUMBNAIL III: DICKINSON

Kettle boiling—
steaming, powering
the molecules
a body
of mostly water
seething
with the energy
of entrapment

no, no, no,

this is no
obvious
clichéd
"I"

The all
corporeal
essence
speaks
to us
in the
uniquely
oblique
stunningly
hauntingly
revenant
like old
proverbs

Truths
wrapped in
a stoned
frenzy.

HILLS

for the men of the 1st Marine Division (Korea)

Driving to Silverton
from Durango, we
survived the mountains—
harrowing hairpin turns
and steep shoulderless
massif grades that plunged
us white-knuckled to
another hilly hairpin turn
and after an anxious hour
a tiny town, a camp
of dollhouses still far
below us, dotting
the valley like some
grand idyllic village
and in the late evening

I finished reading
THE DARKEST SUMMER,
a book mostly about Marines
of the Korean War
and how they survived
hill after bloody hill,
because the war seemed all
about the capturing of this hill
or that hill, and the intense cold
at the Chosin Reservoir
that caused their weapons
to freeze, so that when
thousands of Chinese came
in darkness surrounding them, they
could only toss hand grenades
down the hills or up the hills,
it was always about this hill
or that hill and the maps in
the map rooms of the Generals

on both sides, these hills
all had numbers
and the numbers were piles
of other numbers and they
were like the piles of bodies
that were collected on both sides,
because, they could not bury
them, because the ground was frozen
so they had to make piles of bodies
until they could blow a big grave
into the side of a hill to entomb them.

Warfare has always been intolerable
for the infantry, not like the wars I played
at over forty years ago, a Marine, never
actually capturing a fortified mount
or defending a crucial hill, just enough
war gaming in the barren California
mountains or recon-swimming icy mountains
of Pacific surf off the sands of Coronado Island,
to give me a small possible notion
of what another Marine "Grunt" might
have been feeling in actual combat,
and tonight, alone in my camper
in this scenic Colorado mountain
valley retreat, I cannot escape
those 1st Division Marines
of that historic battling flight
from the icy Chosin Reservoir,
their stories are frozen in my head
and as they were totally surrounded,
they are imbedded in graying hills,
springing up in dark ambushes
of my thoughts; and I remember

my own Drill Instructor preaching, how
fire superiority can overcome any hilly
fortification, explaining how the 1st escaped,
because every Marine is a rifleman

and each time those Jarheads squeezed a trigger
a Chinese soldier went to the cold hard ground,
and I keep thinking that it must have been something
else as well, because they were so outnumbered
and it was so frigid, and there were so many, many
hills, there must have been something burning
deep in the valleys of the very essences
of their individual beings, some other kind
of unique fire superiority.

GHOST HAWK

After William Wenthe's, "Desconsado"

I too remember driving the predawn highways
leaving Amarillo south toward the ebbing
darkness before the blooming pregnant glowing
morning, comfy within the moving blind
of creature comforts; temp controls, corduroy jeans,
Starbucks aroma filling all—all those interior voids
without the yap, yap, yapping of morning radio,
opting for the birthing silence of Texas prairie,

the ghost like shadows flashing by, glimpsed
in the prefaced blood rimmed edging luminosity
of that great body of light destined to come, crowning
the primordial ritual of portents of gilded promise—
smaller dark edged bodies of light beginning to become
fully realized to me by the haunting of *Desconsado*,
a poem fulfilled with that dazed Red-tailed hawk, darting
into the safe cabin of my caffeined morning musings—

I kept scanning the shadows for feathered images diving
or even winged road-kill waving from the center strip,
ascertain that my intense depth of thoughts of them
might somehow become their conjurer, that a hot blooded
stealth of fleeting life might fulfill the outlined promises
of the ghostly figures inhabiting the passing desert vistas,
like some Saint John-like visionary auguring some wildly
dazzling taloned epiphany and behind all, I became vaguely
aware of the engine humming, a dull droning as incessant
as the hive of day-in—day-out of our lives—lives many times
wounded, don't we all wake each day with drumming blood,
with at least a tenuous feathering of the stirring of life's inherent
radiance, rising under a single golden eye, father light pluming hope—

VIEW FROM THE CLIFFS

Nature is a Haunted House—
But Art—a House that tries to be haunted.
        Emily Dickinson

At Timber Cove Inn, two hours north of San Francisco, the raccoons
come to our window after a swim in the rocky garden pools at sunset

and peer into our balcony window from the old oak tree that is twisted
and flailing away from the windy sea. They are looking for handouts

from the untold treasury of travelers: scattered pet food, an orange, perhaps
a scrap of salmon jerky—the air is crisp and rich with that nice mixture

of the bounty of human creature comforts in our encampment and the promising
poignant exotic ocean, blowing in its salted and measured breaths, offering

its own stoked and smoky light, light—bringing our polluted city minds
that sumptuous meat, the essentials for that hungriest of animals—Art.

In the mornings sleek abalone divers can be seen in the shallows far below
undulating like innocent seals fishing the jagged cliffs, spooning the rocks

for that other sweet meat—a month from now we will read news that one
of these morning swimmers will have lost his head to a great white shark—

Emily Dickinson said that a poem should take the reader's head off—
today, where the near crags drop off to the deep Pacific all along Highway 1,

great shadows are turning cold blue tones black and swirling like hunger
in its haunted aqua house, while a thousand miles away, in a makeshift studio

on the edge of the Big Thicket, an artist trades her years of working to capture
the blurred past through Realism for the oblique certainty of the Abstract, diving

again and again into her Dantesque childhood darknesses, finding red renditions
and stunting yellows, black and the uncertainty of gray—she is swirling the many

colors of the truths that had been too raw to capture on a canvas…previously too vivid for memory's chaste channels, fits of splashing colors, violently invading the sweet

sublime of unconscious pretense—finding not *Paradiso*—but, a kind of faith— applying the simple earthly tools of brush and fabric—fearlessly opening portals—

III

THE FRANK GAZE OF WOMEN

THE FRANK GAZE OF WOMEN

After Baudelaire's "Exotic Scent"

Yes, yes, they bestow delights—
    not only in the seedy way
we all know: they plant something
    in the littoral vacancy
and in an instant there is an ineffable
    fire—that forging force
on which so much more depends
    than wheelbarrows & chickens

ORANGE COUNTY APRIL 29, 2005

It is Friday and though I am over a thousand miles away,
I can see you clearly in the east Texas morning
rolling away from my vacant side of the bed
to your feet, as you are compelled
to do every early morning, moving
militarily through the mechanics—creating
another day: the first call of the toilet,
shuffling to the kitchen, water for the kettle,
the daily dolling out of the medicine
to the white counter top, the orbiting shuttle
to our sleepy daughter's bedside
for the exchange of her pills for the small dog
curled resistantly warm under their covers—
    And there you are…there between the oak tree
and the row of dogwoods doing dog duty on your birthday—
what are you thinking today? If I were there, with you
I would not know—behind the physical—the mundane
there is the wonder, the mysterious and unique impulse
that resides in the essence of you—the creation of stunning art
out of the dark world of your haunting subconscious—
I have rarely been able to guess those memories, those thoughts—
even if I were on that common quay—my face inches
from yours, falling, plummeting dizzily into the auburn
framed countenance of your glowing presence—tripping
into the folds of your graceful familiar form, fixed
in wonder on that onyx centering in the greyhound blue eyes,
where that ineffable chalcedonic entity resides and in some
oblique way, *takes dominion of all that surrounds.*

COMFORTER

After turning out the lights,
you curl under the comforter

away from me, as I settle in
behind our half-curved legs.

We are pieced together:
halves of a mid-November moon,

our bodies, an echo—
giving—receiving—yearning

from the vague middle
among thoughtless glands,

as our feet try each on
in the twisted play of loose ends—

loose connections making & breaking
the clumsy vows of dumb extremities.

I remember our children—hugging
their small truths, the war realities

of stuffed animals, the silk of their young lips
against the smooth blanket bindings…safe,

complete.

In the morning the auburn of you orbits
to my bedside and softly descends

with the foggy aroma of ritual tea
or Colombian coffee, falling through

my squinting ellipse, somehow adding
to what seemed complete in that darkest

of patterns. These are not memories
randomly reasoned, nor the flawed promises

made by fickle limbs. These are a few
of the star stitches that burn in the bunting:

a gilded bit of the fabric of what we were,
what was saved without being chosen, folded

neat at the corners, our mellifluent patchwork.

SIXTIES MUSIC

for Susan P.

When the oldies radio station plays,
I Can't Get No Satisfaction...memories

flaming hot, fire-up, flashing sensual scenes—
Susan, waking me—on the family-famous brown

couch in my parent's Rollingwood home, where
I had crashed after partying until the wee hours

following another late night Lifeguard cleaning
session at Barton Springs, our boom box at the max

as we wrestled a fire hose, blasting the basic beginnings
of algae from that ancient limestone creek bottom—she,

stretching her bountiful Scandinavian body smooth
against the length of mine, bringing me alive,

slowly, with the smell of her shampoo, nuzzling
damp morning-hair...and later, that one wild

all night driving of her from Austin to Baytown,
dangerously winding around each other, hands

wanting to be everywhere at once—attempting
to keep my old grey fifty-seven Chevy in tune

with the streaming white lines of the highway,
our heads bobbing, lips all musk and Mick Jaggerish

in the gamy, steaming young music of our bodies.

THE MARRIAGE LOST

for Terry

When everything that could fall

                has fallen

there will always be two hearts hanging

obscure, deep in the gristled harboring breasts

              of us hawks

floating in the constant wind of timeless memories, poised

in the heavy pewtered sky of our two minds—

             there is no true end

to this parting that we have lived with so many years

and now, like two intrepid birds of prey hunting

             in different territories,

we have in common our differences and the blood

of our blithely fey times together—still pumping wild

             in the deep craw

of the ancient machinery of the feathered crafting

of our individual lives since, and residing subdued—

             deep within me

endures the lofty vision from these high altitudes of a time—there

now…that small brown speck in your morning green eyes,

eyes—

that with one blink of the thought of them, a bright portal opens,

a drumming heart—a catch of breath—still singing the sweet

turbulent tones

of our times—swimming in the brine of that one eternal orbit—

suspended—

HISTORIC HOUSES

Walking to Hatfield House
And through, and around, and behind,
We find giant trees with no names,
Scattering shady motifs of their green
Beside the garden walkways.

We move under this cathedral of living thatch,
Each at our own tourist pace, strolling
Through intermittent walls of light
Where branches have failed branches.
You disappear around the last trunk

As I look up to the first fork
Where two trees are formed from one.
I trace the division back down
To the strength of their beginnings,
As I find you again between tree and garden gate.

The narrow path brings our walking together,
Under cool lime tree archways
That square the regiments of neatly
Trimmed shrubs and colorful flowers,
All in their places with faces you recognize—

Iris, pansies, roses...
I keep thinking about the trees,
My arms wanting to reach around them,
Hands and heart flat against the years,
That distance from left middle finer to right,

That someone once said is another
True measure of a man. Our arms
Are pendulous with the rhythm of our walk,
Hands obliging, then touching—dumb
To the promenade and the boxwoods—

Then holding, then letting go—
In their own mirroring ritual,
A revenant miniature played
By lovers' hands of every century,
In the quiet cadence of God spreading seeds
For giant trees with no names.

STEPDAUGHTER

for Laura

The term has always felt clumsy in my mouth
not unlike the relationship at its beginnings—

the tangle of diverse families that creates those awkward
first hugs—so full of the fire of mixed emotions—histories—

I remember the first time I was struck full face by the joyful
blue-green eyes that were plumed in that small face surrounded

by the shock of blondish brown hair…a stunning mane that seemed
much too substantial for a child's head—redolent of thick, lush

texture of the mother's—hair that I remember hurriedly brushing
those early school mornings into shiny bouncing dog-ears—

stunning locks in complicated snares and rats, demanding gentle
concentration, occasionally evoking a snagging yelp and pain

reflected in those eyes—distinctive, subtly different from her mom's,
yet, with the same unusual mesmerizing qualities. Those first blurring years

were the times the awkward nature of the term was truly onomatopoetic
of the relationship—countless hard encounters of miscommunications

and cobbling of minds and wills, and then euphoric discoveries—selfless
moments—genuine feelings of family—the years have passed and like roots

grown in buried tangles under a grand old oak tree, all those complicated
nerve endings, so raw from being torn from their original bodies, have found

their ways to firm new ground, rich loam—step…daugh…ter…the term,
as in introductions, still does not feel correct to my dumb tongue—my daugh…ter,

two smooth syllables combed together as two pigtails woven carefully around
each other—naturally: *I would like you to meet my lovely daughter, Laura*—

THE DANCER

September 11, 2001
for Allie Paige

When she begins moving
her eyes become
pyrotechnic
and her hands
are in a constant state
of graceful articulation,
she is omnipresent will,
her five wispy feet
now appear to
tower,
soulful joy
saying, yes
saying, yes
saying, yes
with every spinning
pirouette.

The hours twirl
into darkness—
centrifugal forces
mixing mundane and monstrous events
of the day—they begin
filing themselves away
in the ash gray
preface to sleep,
she orbits to me,
that lovely moon face
juxtaposing
a good-night kiss
with her nightly promise:
I'll see you in the morning!
an evening ritual
that takes on the new
trappings, trippings,

the inescapable thoughts—
the chilling possibilities
of our naiveté
and the fragility
of our assumptions,
our common
hopes.

SECOND MARRIAGE

This inarticulate wind
always seems to have more
to say, gusty overtones
groaning over eloquence
of sea and sand.

I should be standing
on the steep grassed banks
of Barton Springs:
March breezes seemed more measured
then and the springs tide less, steady,
and sure, reflecting slick green beaches;
predictable lights under the tall
oaks, elm, and pecans
holding on—deep root strong.

I could be moving boxes
under another late March sun,
finding what cannot be thrown away
nor used, stuff for boxes,
internal baggage
to be stored and moved,
carried within its own darkness,
and dropped;
stumbling into—old books
like *Shardik*, found unfinished
page marked with an old faded Polaroid,
black and mostly white,
of a man and woman
at another beach—
and a child holding fast
to the man's leg, anticipating
a wave they could not see…
sand and salt—white.

The wind lulls Kodak-still, like waiting
heavy, like boxes of books exhaling
stale, damp whispers
of a kind of storage.

Then over the blue and the white and the sand
of Galveston, like new
and not unlike wind,
comes this moving—this essence,
this second breath.

FRIED GREEN TOMATOES

for Jeanette Kierbow 1920 - 2005

I cannot recall one conversation I had
with her, just the cool dignified kindnesses
when from Texas I visited her tiny neat
modest Bremen, Georgia, home with photos
of Liberace placed as one might display
important family members or iconic leaders

maybe saints; the sumptuous fried green tomatoes
she introduced to me one day after returning home
for lunch from a morning of sewing on the assembly
line at her life-long Sewell Suit Factory job, yet, her
neatly modest and homely presence, after over five
decades of not having seen her, returns at unexpected

times, her jet black hair and awkwardly attractive
tall rangy angular body with those remarkable eyes,
those icy agates set in that smooth pale oval face,
eyes that seemed to look directly through you
as brown eyes, with all their warm charm
seem never to do…like the difference between

the kindred eyes of dogs and the inescapable
and ineffable combination of chill and thrill
that is stirred subtly deep within our own animal
depths, when unexpectedly one might glance up,
finding his gaze has become locked in—frozen
by the rapt mystical hunter eyes of a stunning cat—

THE VULTURES OF SUMMER VESTIBULES

Hurricane tortured pines
along River Hill
are propped-up, stilled
by an atmosphere,
an aftermath that seems to suppress
songs and wilt small wings
to a fold.

Even saying the word, Houston,
at the dead end of summer
hues without the cry, straining
deep down in the trunk
amidst the darker humidity.

Inside, the dead-eyed ceiling fans
circle ominously, throwing opaque
flutters against the white afternoon
heat, sheet rock corners
the walls, like the last logic
of a drunken poet flying
his narrow sticky stateroom,
before finding only
the cold and darkest chamber
of the congruous body Caribbean.

After a dinner of tortellini, we
sit with the day's surviving
multitudes, bent to TV's flashing
scenes, our fan-cooled thighs
becoming sticky in their many tries,
as we sip at the remnants of tea & ice,
avoiding the lemons with tricky
tongues, trading cool muted sucks
for rapacious demolition of ice,
the universal preservative.

EVIDENCE

When I leave the musk
of your most intimate

auburn presences—
flipping myself out

from our common
flannel cotton sheets—

we ritually secure
ourselves between—

instinctive individual
attempts at preservation

of mutual heat, our
melding moments—

then stumbling out
and up to the rude realities

of the bathroom's
utilities—honking

chrome, cold medicinal
green tiles and stoic toilet—

I sometimes notice
a trace of you, a hair

perhaps, curled along
the sink bowl's curve

or a smear of make-up, cherry
giving blush to the chill—

life to the white sterility—a hint
of the evidence of you—signs

of daily shared presences—proof
of the us…the undisputable: we are—

I think of your complaints of the daily
mess—I am fraught to wash it away.

THE EDIT

Reading a poem to an audience, years
after its having been published
or even revisited, I discovered a word

that should have been another, an edit
that was so obvious to me—the apt word
stealthily entering my consciousness—

I stumbled over it, embarrassingly
losing my train of thought, nervously
shifting my weight, pussyfooting—

my feet doing a little dance, behind
the speaker's stand, my mind
in a state of reorganizational panic,

as when the face of a former lover, emerges
from memory and lightly touches something
strangely new, something ethereal, causing

a deep stabbing regret, a strange mourning of the reality
that has set that old relationship—eyes, mouth, legs, nuances,
into permanent grey fonts of memory: the finality of inky script—

wishing with a small aching remorse that one could at least,
reconnect—to attempt to rewrite the ending, an editing deep
down in the sinews comes—the painful finality of the error—

this flawed personal publication, this misprint in the intimate canon—
I cleared my throat and looked at the audience with a nervous smile,
the false wry smirk of a minimum wage department store clerk, forcing

the move on…the next word, the next line, another poem—Robert Pinsky's
long forgotten comment now comes to mind, "We always publish too soon."

IV

IT'S NOT ABOUT REMEMBERING

IT'S NOT ABOUT REMEMBERING

For Don Williamson

The rare books were on the top floor
of the University of Houston's library,
a building that did not tower
and offered very few windows.
The Gentleman's Magazine offered the view
of England's news events, a medieval
Reader's Digest from which we of Rothman's
seminar were to glean the details
for a paper that would be a proof
of our proper awe for the curiosities
of the period, a report that is lost to me
now, though a fragment of the search
has revenantly appeared at odd
and unexpected times through
these many years—a small news item
      beside the long list of timely
      and mostly untimely deaths: ox cart
      accidents, family ax murders, and the peculiarly
      high instance of suffocations caused by a swelling
      of the celebrants' throats after swallowing unseen
      bees that had lighted without a discernible sound
      onto the froth of the goblets of golden
      mead, perhaps buzzing only as they delivered
      their stingers to the root of the dumb tongues
      in the dark red tomb of the throat
      where, I imagine an odd death rattle duet
      echoing as bodies tumble and worlds change. There

            beside these mostly timeless obituaries
            was the report from Spain: citizens
            from a small mountain valley town
            had experienced a bolting earthquake
            that was so severe their church perched
            over a mile above had been totally destroyed
            as witnessed by the sound of their famous

bronze bells playing the chaotic, melodic finale
as they rolled down the rough, dry gullet
beside the vibrant village green road
to that dark quiet, events reminding me
of that early December evening, sitting
    bone-cold in those common high school
    bleachers of what is now the Stan Slaughter Jr. Gym,
    the clarity of that precise moment of silence
    among the fleshy throng of pre-holiday cheer,
    when Stan Slaughter Sr. could sit no longer sanguine
    next to me, leaping to his feet to thunder down
    the stadium seats to his fallen son, the undefeated
    senior captain of the Blue Devil wrestling team, limp
    in the arms of that dark referee, having broken his neck
    to escape a first pinning in front of an Athletic Director
    father and the stunned crowd, momentarily speechless
    in the square confines of a single horrific thought, trapped
    among the bees, and the bells, and the other dead friends.

SNAPPING IN

And already/nothing remains of the warrior but his weapons/and his gaze.
From Ted Hughes, "The Knight."

That is what my Drill Instructors called it, snapping
in, lying in the prone position for an untold time,

learning the nuances of integrating body and weapon,
arm tightly wrapped, trapped within the rifle sling's

noose, legs spread, elbows flexed into a natural tripod,
eyes searing through the narrow vortex of the battle

sights of an M-1A-1 gas operated, air cooled, semi-
automatic shoulder weapon, squeezing the trigger,

over and over and over and again, wishing for live rounds
to fire, hearing only the crisp jolting snaps of the firing pin

wondering, wandering through the dull soundless voids
of time and thought, occasionally finding melodic notes

of a kind of muscle memory, not unlike years later, standing
in the brisk cold waters of the Snake River, casting over

and over, and over into herds of galloping torrents, white
manes chaotically stampeding mountain stones and Rainbows

and there—and there—and there, something wild, thrashing,
leaping ahead to a murky watery future, returning back, again

having no idea of the time that passes; when attempting
to move, numb, dumb legs, boots finding only slimy smooth

feral stones on the muted face of the yellowish green river
bottom, for an instant, the same hooked heart of the trout

in me flying from one element of air to another, and falling
rock hard, sniped, splayed body instantly awash in the icy, jolting

revelations that must eventually come to the minds of most all
falling bodies, that last flashing white epiphany—and then only

the sounding, drumming eternal waters, the steely tugging tow
of a destined time that must come to us all, of being snapped up—

TEXIAN

Colonel Juan Almonte, Santa Anna's aide, was the first
To call his attention to the heralding of two golden stars
Floating in the familiar field of green, white and red
Over that unlikely mission fort Alamo, small stars
That foreshadowed the larger single searing symbol
Emblazoning our ultimate flag of Texas independence
We fly so proudly today. And each of the banners
That flew over the those many battles, all spoke
With the same unwavering intonation, No!
No, we will not become minions! Imagine with me
The cacophony of these many varied accents,
Of Kentucky, Tennessee, Louisiana, Alabama,
And Tejano, lilting together in the casting throng,
A composition of the most unlikely of battlefield
Symphonies, a timpani for independence.

Walt Whitman wrote in his Leaves,
They were the glory
Of the race of rangers, matchless
With a horse, a rifle, a song, a supper,
Or a courtship, large, turbulent, brave,
Handsome, generous, proud, affectionate,
Bearded, sunburnt, dressed in the free
Costume of hunters, not a single one
Over thirty years of age.

These were the men and boys
Of whom Walt called the jetblack
Sunrise at the last battle Goliad,
The same ebony tinted sun that fell on
The hardened rough hewn clay arch
Of the hallowed battlefield Alamo, where
Within the brawny breastworks of both
That simple chapel complex
And the ragtag men staged within
Was mirrored these same
Uniquely Texian traits.

Texian, Texian, Texian, the word
That soon returned a jetblack siesta
To the soldiers of Santa Anna
In the far flung fields of beach brush,
Mesquite, live oak, and pines
Of the San Jacinto battleground,
Texian, a word immortalized
Now the world over
By the actions of these gallant few.

Yet, these were seemingly ordinary men
With common everyday problems, desires, prejudices,
Fraught with human frailties, not ideal or perfected.
It is said that even General Sam Houston
Years before these momentous days,
Standing deeply depressed perched
Top deck on the river boat Red Rover,
Was saved from a suicidal fall by the sudden
Flash of auburn plumage as an eagle, a Cherokee
Omen foretelling a greatness to come, swooped
Auguring down toward him—

Today we stand with one of Houston's resurrected warriors
So perfectly formed by *Campobella's sword*, ennobled
Amongst these thirteen flags, not an hour's drive north
Of where his grand triumphant destiny brought us ours,
Where the wafting fragrances of salty gulf coast breezes
And the pungent smoke of gun powder sweated the air
That breathed life into the fledging hopeful breast
Of a stately body to come, making legend these hallowed
Winged emblems now fully realized, as our omens,
Their bright feathers forever woven with the blood
Of these many iron willed, uniquely, soulful
Menagerie of men: these Texians.

THE PEOPLE

"Though they became known as Comanches,
they called themselves Nermernuh (The People)."
The Handbook of Texas

Their ancestors thought
the wild flying geese
to be red-eyed white
hounds harrying
damned souls across
the evening skies—

I imagine them standing
in a trance-like state—
seemingly dumbstruck
by the sight of the furious
flights of those many small
hearts beating ruby hope
against plumed breast—

not unlike small flags
flying in formation
behind some unnamed
leader who from afar
looks no different
than the last lagging
harrier waving wildly—

and here, tonight
those spirits fret about
me in midnight's bed
reading—vivid stories
of bloody raids against
the emerging white menace—
clouds of covered wagons—

each crimson episode
another of history's
many tragic tales
of failed preemptions—
the image of that wild gaggle,
so fluent of air and time, returning
again and again and again

the way the scarlet rimmed
eyes of the past always
infiltrate our present—

CANOEING

I

Moving a canoe to water
is hands-on and awkward.
I remember teaching
canoeing
to the Boy Scouts
of Camp Tom Wooten,
where Bee Creek
finds an Austin lake,
boys wrestling aluminum
wedges, plowing crooked paths
to slippery slices of water,
obliquely reminiscent
of an old woman
moving through her beads
to the smooth, flat surface
of the cross,
making earth's ending
a physical release.
Reaching the longer water
requires centering ourselves:
balancing belly-deep
among larger ribs
than any
Adam.

II.

Like the Hopi Indians, we
have our water clans,
yet, our being
is not found
relived
in the reversing
symbols of clouds.
Nor will the schematic
of our past
be discovered, charted

mottle-brown
on some slow moving
hawksbill.
We walk on the wet sand
between the sounding
blue
and the dark
wood
at the foot
in the shadow
of the mountain.
Between the ark
and the armada
the mechanism
of the arm
is defined,
the oar locked
arms of
men.

III

Entering
the water
I found the wisdom
of forms, the giving
and the taking
of bodies
without the torque
of metal
or the tourniquet
of wind—
the way odd
shapes slip
like oval thoughts
into our future,
making
unconscious & precise
the many decisions
of faith.

IV

Lying inside
a grounded canoe
at night, the cold face
of the earth feels
vague as a tumor
through the thin back,
where, like minds, the ribs
are worn
from the inside
out.
This night dreaming
from the overt corners
of a circumsectional
cocoon, sails me
solid as any
Mareotic Lake,
wine or sea,

takes me—
takes me—

from our dark
ellipses,
we all blink
stars

CLARITY

> *"I don't miss the (good old) days (of WWII intelligence work)…*
> *I miss the clarity." C.I.A. Senior Agent Wabash (John Houseman)*
> *"Three Days of the Condor."*

The fact that it may be possible to slip into the United
    States of America
with a small atomic device and explode thousands
    of dreaming children
and thousands of mothers anywhere USA and because
    in the very craw
of my uncompromising zeal for the free will we have valued
    as a people,
juxtaposed against the inescapable instinctive desire to protect,
    to defend—
I long for the old days of clarity—and yet, it would seem
    that the manner
in which the camps have been encamped—extreme left—
    extreme right,
there is a clear reality that is reminiscent of the gaunt eye
    of oppression
that stares blood-shot cold through the years, through
    the many wars
of our fathers and forefathers, iris fixed like some bold
    distinctive emblem
on a flag—fabric of the fleshy garments of the mothers, their
    sleeves empty—
the amputated arms of hope—the mothers that are always
    the ones shot squarely
in the heart when their many soldier sons do their falling in lands
    near and far.
So, I hear myself say we cannot give up freedom for security—
    I lecture to
my family—remember our history…the world has always
    been dangerous—
it may be our turn to maybe pay the price—but then—
    my children's faces—

MIDNIGHT MONTANA

Little Big Horn

Standing
in the middle
of this ancient hallowed
battleground,
my head arched awkwardly
humanly skyward, hands
and heart outstretched
and flat against the icy
north wind, a wind
like the timeless ocean,
knowing no Alpha or Omega
looking upward
like all men, all women
making their stands
in the centering surrounds
of their own personally
flagged arenas—unseen
arrows pinning them
to imperceptible crosses,
my mind is shot through
with the searing thoughts
of the many wars, warriors coming
before me to this very moment
and there it begins
the spinning within
the grand gyre,
my corpse-like ogle
meets the icy ravishing eons:
starry eyes in ebony winged skies,
winds like the myriad of murderous
ravens flapping, flapping
an echo—this must have been
the true sound of the coming
of the Valkyries—

PORTLAND MORNING

for Dash & Joy

Crisp lolling
mountain air
gray squirrels
the true citizens
of the trees
jerking joyously
among redolent
branches of evergreen
black birds bragging
about, strutting
the omnipresence of life
and above my head
a small spider
rehashes its evening
articulating tonight's
smoky traps—scotch
and branch water
come to mind

BOSCOE PERTWEE AND ME

After Umberto Eco

I love the bumper stickers that can be found
in Austin that read, *Under Republicans, Man
Exploits Man*...then the clever saving refrain

that sings, *Under Democrats, It's Just The Opposite*
and I think the most compelling aspect of those
pithy expressions, made in such Will Rogersian

tones, is the discovery allowed to me—to crystallize
my thoughts in all their pure and independent cries
against all those smoky over-organized bureaucratic lies

that blow upon us on a daily basis, oft through the tangle
of laws and the shrill and flashing warped media anglers
that, I must confess, in the final analysis and rabbling rankles

of mind—all bringing me to believe the same as Boscoe Pertwee,
who is said to have adopted the motto in the heat of 1803:
I use to be indecisive, but now, now I am not so sure....

ARCHAIC REFLECTIONS ON BLAKE'S BAPTISM

At St. James Church in the heart of London
the ornate font is found as it was when it was cut
by Gibbon's sword, that likeness for the Lord.

Like the talc that is the clouds above England's
satanic mills, all come together church cold,
polished and still. And still I sit in wonder

of the Lamb and evil's carvings in the plan
as you must have queried at the end
of your first long night, after bending

thoughtfully down, in a love for the light
Your last glimpse in rising might have been
the peaceful floating down of the dove,

but coming up and out and through the night
with a clutch of honed arrows, keen and quivered
gold, your sight wound round the tree of the font

to the end of the devilish curl, and it is there
where the head of a snaked darkness unfurled,
your mental flight surely must have sprung.

THE ETYMOLOGY OF SOUND

There seems to be a discernible alteration, a variance
in the approaching sounds of a civilian helicopter,
and that of a Life Flight or a military craft, Black Hawking
into our psyche—piercing the very visceral essences
of our hunter-gather genes, that fight or flight instinct, adding
to our now learned tribal memories—guttural rasping blades
slicing through the jungles or deserts of any normalcy, chilling
us in an instant with the thought, something has happened, is about
to happen—heads up, heads down—it's in our heads, forever
now, in our heads, it's in our heads—

DISCOVERING SOREN KIERKEGAARD

I have written about this before;
though subtle and more from the oblique,
using the example of one-eyed Charolais,
the way they can move into you
and your horse and without knowing,
take you: horse and rider to the ground.

So, you become the victim
of blind animal power
and your own bridling.

I believe it was like that for him,
a skillful, though forlorn long-rider
attempting to move his countrymen
like some smooth, blond, clumsy herd
to the clear, fenceless green meadow
at the crown of that Dantesque mountain.

I remember how I came to him, where
I first heard his anomalous name.
I have written before, how that image
had ricocheted off a Whitsun star
into my public television…it was simply
a series of documentaries
about famous philosophers, appearing

that serious summer of my personal *earthquake*
in 1975, narrated by Malcom Muggeridge,
whose voice was as soothing and hypnotic
as some grand British father I never had.
Drawing me into the vortex of introspection,
a graying actor that was astral—moving me
in what seemed a glowing
providential way to Soren and his work,
work that was focused and balanced
like the simple axioms of life
on the T-P Ranch, just outside

Marble Falls, where, set against the cleft
Of a brooding hill of squat oak and cedar,
Spinning on its axis, the windmill

skirts an invisible herd, cutting
the stragglers without forcing them, easy
in the whispered wisdom of its working,
though like a woman laboring, embracing her pain,
pain that swells like some ruthless, unabiding truth
in the eternal, starry craw of skulls.

I have tried to say all of this before,
so, here I am again, the rider
drawn to that plodding vehemence
at the vague and dangerous center
of the engine of the herd. I will
read him again, and again, searching
his body for more evidence
of the wounds that might affirm
what I know to be the exquisite clarity
of his noble, sacred scars; then
I know, I will write about this again.

MEMORIES OF CAMP MATHEWS
IN FINNISH RHAPSODY

To be a Marine, you must love your rifle
for a while, at least until you are free
of Drill Instructors, the keepers of the truth of death.

and while you are in this dark state, a boot in boot camp,
you will pray for war every evening, desperate for a fight,
a reason for this purgatorial tie, a proof.

During the scorched inland days, the California summer
skies are rifled with reptilian eyes, sights narrowing
a simple human form, a symbol that could be a child's

sketch of his father or brother, any mother's son
springing up before you, a rapid-fire target
with no discernible face, the face of us all.

MY HERO COUSIN

for Maj. Richard Kierbow

He won no Medal of Honor,
the Distinguished Flying Cross
that does adorn his wall was not given
for one gallant and demonstrative violent action
above and beyond the call, as is often clichéd.
His Cross was received for the ten deployments
and the many scores of missions, flying
the jungled labyrinth of our national nightmare.

He is not returned and buried, too young
among the dead warriors of Arlington's
hallowed grounds or any other veterans
cemetery, though he is nearly buried alive
in the constant barrage of volumes of books
at the Brookhollow Public Library, where
he clocks in every day, again a volunteer,
now piloting tomes to precise landings
on the militarily lined maze of runway shelves,
with the same steady sure handed manner

of the over three hundred missions he made
above those masked jungles of Southeast Asia
forty years ago, with his extraordinary relentless
patience, that unique unassuming heroic trait,
that joining of equal elements of all knowing
wisdom and total ignorance, conserved
in the aerie catalogs of his mind, as certain
as all war's uncertainties, he routinely
climbed into lumbering C-135 tankers
refueling, renewing other fliers or the
mosquito-like FAC's (Forward Air Controllers),
guiding the lethal messages, *missals* sent
down by our fighter jets, daily doing his duty.

So much depends on men such as him,
methodically braving unthinkable possibilities
day after day, hours, minutes, seconds, their lives
checked out with the ever growing risk
of expiration, of never
being returned.

THE LOST GIFT OF TIME & SIGHT

Most of the world is now watching
through a myriad of cold orbiting eyes.

I remember a time lost when there
was only the slow meticulous knitting

of the news, through the many
tellings and writings and readings

coming to us with the slow turnings
of the fabric of days, coming in orbits

of sun and moon, gifting us with time
to check the many stitches for flaws

made by the multitudes of tellers, carrying
on ceaselessly—but now cold aiming needles

like invisible missiles, piercing our airways,
our visions with missals of mayhem, ogres

of mind, invading our hours, days, blaring
screens, urging, hastening us to the precipice,

a cliff of mind, where lemmings leapt, finding
too late, the broken bones of cold, brutal truth—

SOMETIMES THE DARKNESS

for Curtis Coleman

Sometimes the road leads through dark places
Sometimes the darkness is your friend
    "Pacing the Cage," Bruce Cockburn

No one knows what is coming to them
out of time's spin, like fly fishing the muddy
Chama river after heavy rains, rocky snags unseen,

the singer said, *sometimes the darkness*
is your friend and Dylan said, *wise men at their end*
know dark is right and when cancer clouded your way,

you chose to embrace the dreadful dark, the fisherman's
arm continuously apes the arc of the sun, hopeful
in bright streamers adrift in those murky waters, stripping

slowly in over and under the unseen snags, the echoes echo,
sometimes darkness is your friend and when abysmally retching
the feinted cures again and again and again, you came to the unlikely

epiphany of your kindred songster friend, because no one truly
knows what is coming to them out of time's spin, reminding me
of my own poet-mentor friend, proclaiming, again and again, you must

embrace your deepest held pain, as it is your only pure truth deep
within, because *sometimes the darkness is your friend* and as the fly
fisherman marks the arc of day, sometimes a bright fish, emerges
through the gloom
            to strike—thrashing silver-gold
                        on that taut thin line—lightning life.

PUBERTY

The ball rolls right between my legs
and into right-center field.
I am running after it...and yet, I know
it's too late. There is a frog growing
in my pocket...and it squirms
against my leg, I feel
sure that it's going to pee.
I feel a rush of warm—

     God must play center field:
his huge dark glove swallows
and all those cracking
       white-hot shots
          disappear.

The toad has worked itself out
through the hole in my pocket...I shake my leg until
it falls
      back on the side that warts.

All I feel is the velvet stomach and the wanting legs—
I try to find the hole in the pocket as
the slack mouth widens
       like God's glove
          or a muted scream...biting

the air, I am falling,
      falling,
        falling,

following white
and losing, losing
      my head to the smell of something...some
thing that smells of bleeding grass. Later,
in a sleepy warm shower
      Dylan moans
at thirty-three and a third
and somebody keeps turning
       down the sound....

KINDRED

Blindness will only make him see better.
Broken bones will sharpen his wit.
　　　Karl Shapiro

It is with a common horror and awe that we viewed the flashing scenes
and we are stunned into a numbness of our bodies and a daze of minds

with the repetition of it all—I remember the same—another September
and there are the many other days…personal to each of us…the times

we do not have to conjure up…they stick like bad cooking to the dead
pans of our minds, they are the thoughts and the memories that scurry about

like ants kicked from the order of their hilly homes. Yes, I remember
the day that Larry Williams's photo was posted in the *Austin Statesman*

with the same confident expression I had seen countless times caged
under a baseball mask as he sprang up from his catcher's squat to fire

a shot at a stealing base runner. Now, here he was—set jaw—green beret
announcing to his known world that he was through with games, finished

with this life and his name would become the source of rubbings on a long
black wall in Washington…Larry had witnessed the numbness in the dazed

moiré moon faces of a kindred people trapped in anguish, while a clerk
in Saigon before the war went south, and upon his return, had said to me

in a whisper, like a prayer, he had to go back, and this time, he had to be in
the thick of it…he must be part of an answer…action, not awe…Whitman's

body electric, to Hell with the angst, the numbness…embrace the pain…fire the
spirit and go open—eyes wide open to it all—the same wide and kindred

eyes that, perhaps, sent a throng of fellow students to the very vague center—
Kent State University on May 4, 1970—demonstrating their outrage over their country,

the very land that had seeded them with knowledge and the pride
that they had been raised in, a land of gallant freedom fighters,

a peopled history of grand idealistic proportions that somehow now had
seemed mutated: it was as if there had been a stock take over—war became a corporate

boardroom game; where, the moves to erase one or two thousand players
were taken in the cool air conditioned minds of executives and politicians many

thousands of miles from the heat and stench of the jungle factory,
the change from a war of rescue to a daily body count. So they did what they

could and their pointing of single fingers were no match for the rifles;
here's another legacy for us, the pointed single finger in its fall, still fired

the flame that is the inherent instinct of our nation, that burns like a star
in the craw of this new nation, where ever we single souls abide, we are steeped in

the parables found in our many sacred stories even though
our grand monumental buildings may fall to the warped logic of our enemies; and

this cornucopia of a planet that we so treasure, may turn on us,
like some old jaded lover, bringing on us all matter of venal apocalyptic

weathering pain that rivals the Old Testament curses—*We the People*—
do not sit long sanguine on the comfort of our couches before the gnashing media

poor-sayers or dig head-holes of rationale to bury our worst fears in—
We the People—are on the march, on the move from our every beach, plain, forest,

hill, or cove, on the phone with our support, in the mail with our
personal treasures, we are on the many roads and byways with our pyrotechnic

presences, in the hot stink of it with our time and boundless talents—
unleashed and on the roll—the bright points of individual suns are burning
white hot—wild

and true in every audacious American breast—*We the People*—are truly—
omnipotent—

HANDBALL

The empty salt-lick of a room
is only disturbed by a polished

raft of birdless Maplewood, soon
To be shrieking at our shoes.

The walls, white without padding,
do not resemble sails squared

by corners, they are too plain
for any mctaphor.

The game of fives is what moves
within these walls: a small bouncy

blue ball is the pseudonym.
We stoop to enter this heady

framed mausoleum through a door-like
hatch…we are tricky-latched in

and for a wonderful while,
we are that blue stone's

own smooth puppets—
we follow, like blind prize fighters,

swinging, swinging, swinging,
not listening to anything

but the smacking sound
of some animal's last wet skin

and our handler's thumping plan
again, and again, and again—

GOOD FRIDAY

I

I am thinking of my sister Patricia
this Friday before Good Friday,
as always, her brown moon eyes rising
out of another year's memories, falling
into the slow contemplations
that circumscribe my thoughts, memories
that must be reviewed like some celestial truth
every holy week.

According to my mother,
at eight years of age Patricia
was the brightest of we four children.
I imagine her eyes then: the snap,
the spark they must have shown
anticipating Easter weekend.
Northcross Shopping Center
was within sight of our backyard
across the vacant spring field
of milkweed and scrub grass
that was to soon become
Lamar Junior High's playground.
We had made the trip across the field,
running across the busy Burnet Road
countless times.

> *Y'all hold each other's hands and look*
> *both ways before crossin'…you hear me, David?*

I don't know why I didn't go with them
to buy Easter candy that Friday.
I cannot recall the sirens or how
I learned of the accident. I only remember
being on my knees at the foot
of my parent's bed, praying

the prayers of a ten year old
for the life of a little sister,
making promises I could not keep.

She was in a coma for months,
after three brain operations,
she was still not expected to
survive...a part of her didn't.
They always said that it was the rocket
hood ornament of a fifties model Buick....

II

Good Friday gray mutes
veins of red and green: stains
of the glass butterfly
that floats in the corner
of my bedroom window.
Nancy says that Good Fridays
are always overcast, cloaked
in gray; that Easters end up
bright and sunny. It pleases her
to think of these days as being arrayed
as her priest: auguring those days
of blood and sun...I am thinking
of my sister, Patricia, she is crossing
the vast green field that separates
our home on Shoalwood Blvd. from the busy
Burnet Road & Northcross Shopping Center;
where, the Big Bear Supermarket holds the visions
the visions that are a child's Easter, where
the flesh of eggs is always marshmallow sweet,
their hard white shrouds arrayed colorfully
in the habits of make-believe seasons
and chocolate bunnies with their dark hollow heads
wait like their many blood-filled brothers: stilled
on the center stripe of the high traffic shopping lanes,
frozen by the flashing silver eloquence of mid-day grills

and windy mechanical groans, their hollow heads
destined to know in an horrific instant everything
about teeth and chrome.

III

Nancy's prophecy is fulfilled: the stained glass butterfly
is floating in the bright bliss of a blue Easter sky.
I envision my sister, Patricia, in San Antonio
in her small apartment, feeding breakfast to Bela,
her two year old daughter, her miracle child.

Patricia and her Doctor had believed Bela
to be a reoccurring kidney ailment. After all,
Patricia was well over forty; thought to be barren
because of the months of darkness—she was six months
pregnant…my mother gasped over the telephone,

David, it's a miracle of God!

Three months later Bela was born…on Good Friday.

This East sun will fall into the surviving pines
that stands like stoic pedestrians across my driveway.
with unabiding glee of a child's first enlightenment, light
will breach the skull of the earth, parting, imparting,
rootless, wonderful spontaneous laughter throwing
an enlarged silhouette of a butterfly onto the pillows
of our bed, where later, my own earth-brown iris will fall
and then rise, darting across an airy field, trying
a kind of sky, with this young blush of light
dotting that darkest of paths.

PEACE

Our world continues to orbit to tomorrow's light
and our world keeps turning then to darkness

and there, and there again—is that stillest point,
where light dissolves into total darkness, and there

again, dark begins its turning to absolute radiance
and we all yearn for that stillest point of awareness,

where we are one with the illuminating light,
where we are one with the mystery of darkness,

for we are seeds—in the image of the First Mover,
our very atoms imbued with the essence—Eternity

and we are as accustomed to moving to the light
as we are familiar with moving to the darkness

and though we long so for that stillest moment
we will not arrive at that genuine point of peace

while we remain in this daily turning to light, to inky darkness
for we are an inseparable element of this great gyratory

rotating, and turning in the unique orbits of our own
personal journeys, because the true Peace within us all

is not finished with itself—and until we are truly aligned
with the turning to that still point of light, to the darkness,

until we are perfected, the world will keep turning to darkness
for us and the world will keep turning to light, turning to light—

for we are singularly the plantings, the seeds of ultimate Peace.

KITES

Death is such an awesome
experience that it takes
your breath totally away.

I wish for this poem
to be the antithesis, under
stated, even modest

like simply breathing,
yet, indispensable
like the brisk breezes

holding colorful sails
against clichéd blue skies
or the breath that sends

aloft the many shaped lively kites
like student aspirations, dreams
tied to the determined fists of hearts

with the almost imperceptible strings
of hope, perhaps, one climbing a bit higher
with the small wind of this poem.

I wish this poem to breathe

LOSING SIGHT

A stroke should be drama—surely pain—
I thought it just a wink that went wrong,
like morning eyes, a temporary blurring
shadow, a problem with the mechanism
a glitch with the softest part of the hardware.
A small error that surely could be corrected
with wonder drugs, perhaps super eye drops
or a precise laser shot to the correct nerve.

It was a blink
that changed
everything
leaving me
with no peripheral
vision.

That I could lose sight forever
with such nefarious subtlety,
makes me wonder in random moments
at all that might have been lost to me,
in that same innocuous fashion,
much of which I didn't even realize
had been missing—
        the many hours, days, years,
precious minutes and seconds, so many
of my children's lived moments, while
the dark shadow of personal ambition moved
me through thunderous life, spending
countless times squandered—now embarrassing attempts
to pass the many pointless, worldly eye exams, to find
some charted societal recognition—a vision of success,
sadly living my every days with that one benign blind spot.

MY PREVIOUSLY OWNED SON

for Robert Cunningham

"I'll be watching you…."
        Sting

Like me, and most men I know, he would wish
his poem to have a glib title, something
deflecting, as we all usually redirect any angst
that life might have offered up to us
with humor and; what our many pscho-
analyst family members would term,
stuffing it, and for him there must certainly be
a musical reference of some meaningful nature,

after all, it is surely the sublime timbres of his mind
that have truly defined the essence of the young man,
and travel, perhaps a large ship, though not the Aggie
one, where he spent his first summer at sea, in searching
himself and other strange geographies, a discoverer—
because, for him, it has always been about revelations

for the man I have been watching since the year
of his tenth birthday, when I first met full face
that smiling Dutch boy look of promise, pure, raw hope
and a palpable trust, despite all that he had witnessed
in his small version of the world. Years later, I remember
a face grown twice as old, in a hospital bed, the heart tests,
and we, having been told by the Doctor, must inform him
of his grave and hopeless condition, and as we did so,
with a parent's acute agony, that same face stared
back at us with complete disbelief, saying, *Oh, that's bull
shit! No way! No way!* And by day's end, we learned, yes,
in some miraculous way, the heart had begun to recover
as if willed by the sheer power of that irrepressible hope,
inexplicably, creating his own realities and now, after all

these many years of watching, I know that his heart
is a unique instrument of music, with its own rhythms
and it is also a kind of boat that carries, him and those
he loves and any of life's voyagers in its wakes, glees
of discoveries of what may be found in those darkest
of destinations that we must all enter, while traversing
life's adventurous destinies with the ever present underside
of most any adversities, that simple and healing potion.

I WOULD GIVE YOU THE SINGLE STRAWBERRY

Not because it is the end of May: the season—
or that in the 17th Century William Butler said,

It is doubtless God could have made a better berry,
but doubtless God never did; or that the delicate

uniquely heart-shaped berry has been heralded
through the ages as a symbol of purity, passion

and healing; or because of Shakespeare's adornment
of Desdemona's hankie; or that Madame Tallien

of Napoleon's court would crush 22 pounds in a fine
basin and bathe in the glory of the luscious ruby juices;

nor because of its shape and color, it was the symbol
for Venus: Goddess of Love; or that it was widely held

by Romans to alleviate symptoms of melancholy, fainting,
kidney stones, halitosis, attacks of gout, liver and spleen;

not even the legend that if you are lucky enough
to have a double berry and share it with one

of the opposite sex, surely true love will follow;
not even that they are the only fruit carrying their seeds

boldly on the outside like the regality of knights of olde.
I would give you the single strawberry as a kind of communion

offered in recognition, remembrance and celebration of our brotherly
and sisterly spirits; moreover, as a reminder: strawberries are not harvested

with machines, their small bodies being so very delicate, human hands
must carefully harvest each berry; and as we savor it, let us meditate together on the visions

of the multitude of pickers—people like you and me—bending
under brutal sun in the rote of work, taking each unique berry

with measured grace, with reverent aplomb—I would give you
a single strawberry because, despite all that has perished

and been lost the past year, we
have lived to see…to taste another glorious spring!

V

COLOR OF MOURNING

COLOR OF MOURNING

She awakened to Texas summer bright
in her eyes, throwing on a new yellow
robe, she dragged her body into the kitchen
to make coffee which she dug from a deep
yellow decanter. Awareness steeps through
the heart beating perks, her eyes fall on the child's
drawing that was stuck on the refrigerator door,
a yellow duck swimming on deep dark
water under another bloody sun brimming
with amber iris—Iris, goddess of the rainbow,
adding to the litany of golden messengers, all
bringing to her mind the dress, the yellow
dress that she had given to her niece
for her fifth birthday, the sweet lemon
yellow dress that the child delighted in so
that today she was to be buried in it—the sanctuary
of the summer kitchen felt unusually cold
as she cracked a single egg, spilling
carefully the delicate yoke onto melting butter
thinking, yellow—yellow—
yellow should not feel like this.

THEY

for Harry Dazey

Now that we know that Harry has Alzheimer's
we catch ourselves wondering out loud

about our own memories, searching
for that small void in our understanding

of time's continuum. This cruel wound
that delicately as some evil surgeon unseals

the mute gray bindings that hold
ineffably the inventory of a life,

stuns us again and again with horrific wonder,
leaving us with facial expressions, not unlike his,

as he turns his bent spade, again and again,
like some blind farmer through

the rough weed filled furrows
of recollection and recognition.

At the Garden Café, Ruth stately still,
rotely asks him in that wifely way:

Would you like tea or coffee, Harry?
Harry, do you want tea...or coffee?

...then the realization...*oh...oh, give him tea.*
An acquaintance happens by the table,

and Ruth graciously, dutifully introduces her
to Harry, who, as always, smiles affably

and responds, I am not really here,
you know. Later, I accompany him

to the men's room, where he becomes confused
and begins to wash his hands before entering

the small dark stall with its endless
roll of blank white sheets of paper.

Standing before the sink, he stares
with what appears to be rapt erudition into the mirror

and whispers in that familiar, gentle fatherly tone,
He wants to come back you know; he wants to come back

and they—they won't let him.

LAKE LADY DANCING ON THE HILL

for Shirley Schwaller 1946-2007

Above the south shores of Lake Travis
she moves in the dawn that is breaking
over the railings of the house that clings
to the ancient limestone cliffs—she is the deep
and complex aroma of a dark, rich coffee held
in both hands against gusts of wind that have carried
a chill across the water, a body so deep and blue
that it captures all the light intense morning sun
can send against the hill country valley fortified
with green plumes of Texas plant life barricading
the giant furrow—the sides of the vast aqua catacombs.
Like that steady open vein that flows below, she will
be still moving in the evening that has broken over
that same ornamental ironwork for years, saving
the crow's watch of a porch that juts artfully from
the brow of the hillside she loved, she is this grand house
that will always bring joy to the hearts of memory—
to those lucky travelers that found themselves in her
respiteful inn of light and laughter for a day, or maybe
a weekend—for an, *anytime*—for she is the mother of joy,
she is the girl dancing and singing glory on the hill top
high above the water that like her mind, looking so calm
on the surface, is always eternally sounding our depths,
she is that energy that makes all that surrounds resound.

INSCAPING THE STORM

for Father Hubert Kealy (1938-2010)
after Paul Mariani's Gerard Manley Hopkins: A Life

He once said to me, if the Christ
splendor had not seduced him,
he would have given himself
to the Lady Literature, his mind
to happily spin in the sweet Irish
gyre of his genes—his heart of mind
is still and forever will be pierced
by Gerard's grandeur, his body joyfully
churning with the oceans of inscapes
filled with blessed blood, propelling,
priming life's profundities through
the ardent aspect of a saintly eye,
and just as now, I remember him

standing tall on the very anniversary
of Hopkins' vows, a stormy Feast Day
of the Assumption, he is at the wheel
of the holy galleon, Sacred Heart Church
and he—is—the eye in pandemonium,
like that bold lioness nun of the doomed
Deutschland, he centers himself
in the Mass, our majestic main mast
cloaked in the sails of his creed,
flying our colors proud, despite
the keening cancerous plague,
the waves of chemo nausea,
the agonizing baneful babble—all
landings within his sight fraught
with the wrecking rocks of ruin, yet
he stands amidst the brunt of it, his frail
alb-clad jib raised—strong on high, chevying
chaotic, chthonic born winds, proclaiming
against all darkness, to all above, all below
and to us huddled around on hallowed deck,

This is my body...this is my blood....

CHALLENGE COURT

For Fred Copeland

In the Challenge Court you have no set partner
and the matches come to you like blind dates

with their many unexpected quirks: odd
styles of service, surprise shots and strange

nuances that bring mystery and a certain
edgy anticipation to every game. It is there

that I often found him with his Ex-Marine handshake
and congenial look-you-in-the-eye smile...before and after

our play. He was the gentleman hunter—when you
became his game, his style was a kind of stalking.

I remember my old Austin friend and partner, Jim Sellers
with his awesome animal athleticism—relentlessly attacking

the ball straight on with stunning velocity, as if it were
some huge and lethal insect, swatting it time and time again,

anticipating its geometric flight like some expert Entomologist
gone mad, most volleys ending in dramatic and resounding

bottom board kill shots, whereas, Fred's style was as smooth
and confident as his demeanor and his ageless pompadour,

only with fisted waves, curls, and left hooks—deceptively deadly
and yet, not extreme, not like "Captain Hook" Reeve, with his jaw-

drop—ball hopping, Fred's way was subtle...like some cancer
that after being diagnosed in the first prophetic shots brought predictable

and deadly ends to the remaining volleys. That one such as he,
with such control was downed with that single shot to the heart

is not ironic, there is no poetry to our loss—there is only the stillness
of that quiet valve: the Handball Challenge Court—waiting—

in the Downtown YMCA in the heart of Houston's tangle
of arteries and the question that comes to mind every time

I now stoop through the small passageway to begin
another challenge match: How could a totally empty

20x40x20 room with all white walls seem more vacant,
yet, fertile of mind, like some primitive Rothko sanctuary?

FLYING TO MY FATHER

Flying into Florida, the dusty lights
of the porthole fall into earthen galaxies, thickening
white like memory, reflections
play off the realities of St. Petersburg,
as I wonder at the falling from the absence
of all colors to their many presences.

The airport is full of hollow eye, heavy
with their unique waitings, and I follow
luggage signs, looking for that familiar
barrel chest with its invisible wheezing.
Finding you in the main terminal, we hug
in our clumsy way, handshake trapped
like manhood between us. At times like these

I always remember your startled face
the first time I hugged you as a man, when
I left for the Marines. Things were more
desperate then. The flying years have eased
us together, our reunions, somehow
allowing me to embrace my future self.
After an evening of catching up trailed
us to a wondering goodnight, the next day
we breakfast late with predictable conversation

and more sitting. Later at the beach, I feel
I must run, away, down that endless earth-line
that always returns to where it began. Jogging
between the water and the starkness of condo
conversions, my mind begins—

All those verses about beaches—
and the word about the sand grind
boringly in—whiting—
there is a lot of white here.
On this narrow way bleached
dollars crushed like cracker against
water's crest: grit

Like that which mends the angles of bricks,
those building blocks of white on the strand,
where inside the many fathers
grown whole, waiting under white hair
smiling tan-tough smiles with synthetic
teeth, that are an assonance of their many reasons
as there are no new words, only silent negotiations.

SPEECHLESS

I found my father that late December morning,
as if he had just lain down to sleep, hands
at his side, right hand holding his always present
asthma spray, dull eyes seeming to ponder the tiles above
as if absently looking for familiar shapes to pass
the time, like he taught us to do with the clouds
on those long, infrequent West Texas road trips.
He would take us for a week or so, to allow
Mother a summer break and help us to understand
a rag salesman's life without having to actually speak.

I found my mother after penning a poem articulating
the difficulty I had experienced writing about her—she
was kneeling, dressed for bed, into her small glowing
bathroom tub that received her petite frame
like a large porcelain sea shell with its life half in—
half out—her face pressed flat to the surface, as if
she were listening to some astonishing sound—blush
of crimson whispering from her mouth—nothing
in her entire life ever could keep her speechless.

BRIDGEWELD

for Wesley Farris

We drove his trucks to my first
bridge job. Early Austin morning
rear-viewed with the sun, as we
bounced in tandem to the coastline
light. That Kemah bridge opened
like an old fold-up couch, creaking
a yawn from the earlies. The cement
shoes on the new span towered
over the rickety cross-over
like giant grave markers.
The metal in Wesley's smile
was golden. The spittle
of another's fiery arch had left teeth
marks on most of his shirts.
When his teeth were hooded, thick
fingers worried his head and plucked
at thinning eyebrows over scared blue
eyes. Processions passed under us
like blinks, never seeing our work
or the welding. Walking on I-beams
before the welding made the flat step
of steel push back my younger boots,
making sure I feel the still moments
between, like a first dance two-step.
By summer's end, balance was a breathing.
Now, years later, Wesley's step is a waltz
bringing gaps in a high way, flux
of memory burned to a dust, smoothing
the weld.

ROOTS

for Hasten Kierbow

They reminded me of the limbs
of the aged—tree roots
erupting from the solar plexus
of the Austrian hillside, veins
bulging blue in their final cycling
through my grandfather's plateaus
of rumpled white, gripless pain.

We left the trail to be close
to them. Helping each other
hand over step, over hand—up
steep clay streaked inclines
to touch their articulate clinging—
clutching to them, to the mountain,
to each other, to the moment,
defying gravity and other forces

unseen…quiet erosions, subtle
as a creeping cycle of sun
and inescapable as shrugs of wind
jerking ragged shrouds of snow
from cathedrals of evergreen
to barren mountain shoulders, shaded
surreal blue above Innsbruck's
innocent organization of morning.

DISCOVERY

for Howard Moss

We all, despite our coy demeanors,
held out hopes that we would be
his Houston discovery.
I was less diffident, asking him to lunch
before his lecture on Emily,
to discuss a handful of my poems
with modern poets as my theme.
        Howard Moss, after a lunch
of turkey & pumpernickel
mixed with conversations
about my one failed poems, titled
Pound, Eliot, Frost,
and *Whitman*, the one
that, *held some promise,*
the horrors of Houston's
weather and traffic, the pure joys
living in London, and No, I am not kin
to the marvelous New York dancer
of the same name—I insisted on paying
with a weak joke about obligation
as a tactic for publication, he stumbled
out of the University of Houston Hilton,
his hands braced over his head
against the overwhelming submissions
of noon sun, stunned
by the kite-like colors, seemingly pinned
like a butterfly to a vast blue cliché, discovering
his first ultra-light aircraft—*What is it? It's marvelous,*
really marvelous—floating high as hopes
over the tombstone gray Cullen Building, appearing
like some exotic bird for poem from South America
flying into his head like new life from Elizabeth—
        The next day, falling ill,
he would fly home to New York City, discovering
there his own peerless place
in death's dark helmet.

REMEMBERING ASHLEY MICHELLE

for the Donnie & Linda Parsons Family

Robert F. Kennedy is often quoted: *There are those*
   who look at the things
the way they are and ask, why? I dream of things
   that never were
and ask, why not? That small piece of trivia emerged
   from some lost cells
in my brain as I searched the old family Bible
   for the correct spelling
and reassurance of the memory of your name. This year
   my youngest
Allie Paige left for college and the house became empty
   as an abandoned
cradle...not a nest, as the symbol is so often applied...
   it is a question
instead of the furniture of a life not realizing its creative purposes
   anymore.
Consider the invisible skyscrapers, soaring transparent
   in the dull, dead
haze of an early evening, without the body, the body of work
   that their
young dead architects failed to live long enough to design,
   the many
lost moments of passage a parent makes with their child
   on the journey
creating the architecture of a life...I confess, the numbers of times
   I've thought
of the many missed moments, the lost possibilities of your life
   is so seldom
as to be an embarrassment to me now, as I sit in the quiet, vacant
   living room,
the crib of my own home, a structure full of the rich memories
   of a thousand

clichéd moments with my now grown children and the thought
    of you, Ashley
with your mom and dad and the many poignant parallel moments
    never made
whole, the soaring invisible bodies of work that remain unrealized,
    yet still
remain, persisting as stars in the deep craw of our minds, dots
    of light that lay unconnected.

SPRING SUICIDE

In spring the cars of light begin their trips, plotting
    Their way through thin grey solenoids

Of fall, where tall shadows have been eclipsed
    And dappled skins of green reclaim the voids.

Winter leaves town dragging its dark, soiled pale
    And a sixties Chevy rubbers the winding trails

Of the cold shoulders of Mount Bonnell, leaning
    Into the spin high above Bee Creek, the wind, no rail—

Through safety glass appears a lost young smile
    Winslow Pratt's red-faced Howdy Doody simile

Speeding through the hair-pin turn, flying
    Into my poem as my first deathly dark memory.

TRAIL MARKERS

for Jack Wilkes

Every first Monday of the month
you would pick us up, 6:30 P.M. sharp

for Boy Scout meetings: Troop 1
at the O. Henry Junior High gym,

my school, the same space I learned
to dance in socks, doing the two-step,

and how basketball was a kind of dance
from five foot tall, Coach Herman Wiese.

My traveling salesman Dad never being home,
your zeal was the only thing that kept me

in Scouts, you made it so easy, always
picking me up for meetings, weekend camps

and then helping me in securing a summer job
teaching Canoeing and Rowing at Camp

Tom Wooten. I remember how you would
go out before our camping trips and leave

Indian trail markers for us to find and follow
and how to make wild berry tea and survive

eating plants and grubs. Time and again, I
have found aspects of the ideal man in small

examples you planted in my head; in five decades
I never thought of you not surviving anything.

You were the most honest, self-resourceful man
I had ever known. I can see you now, tanned,

tall and slim with graying temples, impeccable,
Atticus Finch in a Scout uniform with your

ever present Eagle Badge and knee socks.
After the Scout meetings, we would always
play a pick-up game of round ball, while

you would pack up the scout stuff and re-clean
what we had missed in our half-hearted attempts,

though firm, you never ranted or raised your voice.
On the way home we would frequently stop

at Scotty's Bakery, where I would buy a dozen
hot, out of the vat glazed donuts and wolf down

the entire bag before being dropped off,
after all these years, I can still feel

the huge knot of sugar, grease, and dough
tightening my gut, not unlike the feeling

I had when my old, fellow Scout Bert told me
you were gone and I had missed your funeral,

and yet, even if I had been there, it would have
been too late to tell you what I regret never saying,

simply, Thanks, Mr. Wilkes, I do not know who
I would have become without having known you

and after all these years, I am still discovering myself
in memories of your many edifying ways, trail markers.

WHEEL WELL

and I am sleepily driving Allie Page to school
and I am there in the organized chaos of the high school
        parking lot
and the students and parents and teachers and campus police
        are all
about the business of solving the puzzle of the many cars
        and students
advancing on the new day at this institution of tomorrows
        and my daughter
climbs out of the truck to join the throng moving
        like communicants
to the alter of the church of high school education
        and out of the corner
of my eye a very young grey kitten is dashing under
        around and through
the many anonymous sleepy blind faces in the cars and trucks
        and those standing
on the sidewalks and no one sees the frantic little feline stall
        under the sky blue
SUV with the unawares father like me edging his truck and mind
        with the stops
and starts of the long queue and the small grey of the kitten
        disappears up
and into the dark womb of the driver's side front wheel
        well and the driver
pulls forward just a turn and there is the kitten rotating
        to become a dead gray
smudge and I am looking to see if anyone else has witnessed
        this and there is no one
and something is curling into the fetal position in
        the well of my mind
and I am thinking: I had no time to do anything and it is no one's fault
        and I am thinking
how my friend Gene always says that everyone he meets in the day
        is a special appointment
made by God and I am driving back home to my coffee
        and my bagel with crème cheese

and my blood pressure medicine and my vitamins and my fish oil
    and the *Houston Chronicle*
and I will again check the sports first and glance at the Obituaries
    and settle in to the Crosswords
and I will watch CNN for the latest disaster spinning
    out of control and the day will begin
filling up with the many thoughts and tasks—the gotta-do's—
    and the day will continue to turn
and I will be thinking about all the many wheels—wheels within
    the Great Wheel—how we are all
on this sphere that is rotating like a great unstoppable and unawares wheel
    that darkest of wombs and....

KNOWING TEXAS (2012)

for Cpl. Joseph D. Logan

Outside Abilene under huge sky filled fields
of the family owned cotton farm, an only son
has come back home from a life lived in
the now burn-dotted rolling verdant hill country
and the drought drudged lakes and streams
of an inexorable bustling eclectic Austin metropolis
and he is kicking the inherited dusty furrows
like the tires of some old familiar used car
with comforting boots that still fit after thirty-
some-odd years, while on the very lush edge
of the Big Thicket forest, over 400 miles southeast,
an artist is perched cozy in her small town tree
house of a studio, painting with joyful wonder
a black capped chickadee, a bird she had never
noticed before, living cloaked for years in the deep
green shadows of lofty pines, brush, and scrub oak, while
further south, there is a man milling live oaks washed
dead with one sweep of hurricane seas gone in-
land, his ruddy hands working smooth the track
of timber destined to sail the very deadly sea
that had abruptly stopped its green prodigious
life on the Galveston strand, while further south
a padre lights candles on the altar of an old Spanish
church in Ft. Stockton, as he thinks of his own home village
thousands of miles away in India just south of Bombay,
Texas flora, fauna and people are so prodigiously
diverse that one may never live long enough
to truly know them all—this month we buried
a young Marine come home to the Sam Houston
Cemetery in Willis with only 22 years of knowing.

SOUNDING

Tonight, three gray whales are bobbing for air,
feathering up through centuries of ice,
chanting toward the light shades of shadow

that mark a ragged, scarring circle of sky.
Television tells me that one of the three
ghostly figures is very young, perhaps a son.

I click the set off,
and I move from Point Barrow, Alaska,
to our kitchen, the last muted sounds

of the ceiling fan's circling fades
from the living room, drowning
in the omnipresent silence—I think of my children

all sleeping as I left them, curled around
cordless air in small hugs of self—looking
down into the sink, my face mutates

in the reflections of stainless steel—
like opening my eyes under deep, clear water
and finding some twisted, familiar face

staring back. Turning on the tap, I wait
as the small round light at the end
where the only sound

is the predictable exhaling escapes
and the inevitable gushing falls
to the draining…to a larger dark.

The heated water kicks in—emerges
blunt—a subtle change in pitch: a fission
born by quickening of atoms—that tiny life.

A sound so slight as to have been lost
to me the many years before this very moment.
I have heard it said that sound, once born,

swims in air immortal, circling
within its own sphere of existence,
bobbing through timeless atmospheres

that are deep and clear, like some holy water—
atmospheres that hold the spawning tympanum
of every faint first breath, every straining lonely

last gasp and every mourning parent's gnashing, "No!"
Standing in the center of this simple kitchen, for the first time
in over forty years of my sloping for light—I am certain

Truman was wrong, we were wrong, and the horror—
at that time, I would have done the same thing.

EDITING SKY

for Jame C. Kennedy

I can see you there at your place
on Great Oaks Parkway,
a ten year old half-breed boy
all barked over in seventy-five
years of skin. You are writing me
the letter about living and dying,
cancer, and the new medicine men,
they're cutting you all up, and then
the bloodless scalping.

I think of our Comanche mother
rubbing you raw with whitewash & pumice.
In trying to bleach herself out of your
smooth tailored skin, you became an even
redder half-Irish. Even before then, blood
had welled 'round your high cheekbone firmly
pressed to the hardwood stock, lightly butted
with the single shot from a small bore
Twenty-two. Your first buck's last leap

for that little space of blue between
Spanish Oaks clinging to the hill country
roll brought you both down to earth.
Like some men, trees edit what we know
of the sky. A great oak is falling
to steel crutches in its reaching
from the steep grassed banks
of Barton Springs to the other side.
You would know the tree.

It was our place by the deep: a cold, dark
blue hole in the fault line, the source
of our being there. One day we took turns
diving to see how close we could swim to that gush
of silent thundering. Then we would burst

to the surface gasping for the means, our
bodies spring-blasted, a tingling, newbornish sting.
Like survivors, we would crawl out under our tree
and lie like bacon on the sun-pebbled walk, dripping

while I hoped for one of your stories
about Indians, being a G-man, just anything.
I would then climb up to ride that smooth
saddleless girth, before it was packed with cement,
pretending I was Indian, too. I don't think you
ever knew how hard I rode that old tree
never reaching the other side. Today, if I could
I would leap up, straddling that gnarled,
crippled old steed—

borrowing God's spurs like stars,
we would buck loose from the earth.
Picking you up out of that blanket
of skin, sleek we would ride—high—

ride the bark off that old paint
clear to the other side. Then
just as that fickle spring's reflection
began cooling off the sky, we three—
we would dive—

NOTES:

EDITING SKY: Dedicated to James C. Kennedy

MEMORIES OF CAMP MATHEWS: Where Marines received
rifle training in the Sixties.

LIFEGUARD: Disch Field, not to be confused with Disch-Falk
Field, was located on Barton Springs Rd., one block east of
Lamar Blvd. and was used by the Austin Pioneers, a minor
league team of the Fifties & Sixties. The field was torn down
in the Sixties.

THEY: Dedicated to Harry Dazey.

RE-RESURRECTION: Dedicated to the members of the Marine
and SEAL school command who trained me at the Recon-
naissance Scout Swimmer School at the Naval Amphibious
Base, Coronado, Calif., later losing their lives in Vietnam.

CANOEING: Mareotic Lake/Sea is site of the vision of the human
soul in Shelly's, *The Witch of Atlas* and appeared in Yeats's,
Under Ben Bullbin.

AUSTIN RELATIVITY: For the Barton Springs Lifeguards of the
sixties, especially, Fred Hanna, Eddie Peterson, and Bobby Jones.

CHALLENGE COURT: For Fred Copeland, lost to a heart attack
at the Houston Downtown YMCA, Court 10

KITES: Originally the title was "Occasion." The poem was
composed at the request of the student editors of *SWIRL:
Lone Star College Literary & Arts Journal* for their 2008-2009 is-
sue, which they dedicated to me: a high and humbling honor.

TEXIAN: *TEXIAN* was composed in response to a request from
the City of Conroe & Lone Star Monument & Texas Historical
Flag Park Committee, to be read at the opening, unveiling
ceremonies on the 175th anniversary of the Battle of San
Jacinto, April 21, 2011.

1. References to Col. Juan Nepomuceno Almonte were found in the *Texian Iliad* (University of Texas Press) by Stephen L. Hardin.

2. References to Sam Houston's encounter with the eagle on The Red Rover were found in *Sam Houston* (University of Oklahoma Press), James L. Haley's biography.

3. Craig Campobella is the sculptor of the statue of The Texian centered in the The Lone Star Monument and Historical Flag Park in Conroe, Texas.

HILLS: I am appreciative of Bill Sloan and his fine book *The Darkest Summer*, detailing the battles by the United States Marines that saved South Korea.

MARRIAGE LOST: For Dr. Terry Parsons Smith. The first line is taken from the Ted Hughes poem, "The Guide."

STEPDAUGHTER: Dedicated to Laura Doehrman

INSCAPING THE STORM: Dedicated to Father Hubert Kealy 1938-2010

LAKE LADY DANCING ON THE HILL: Dedicated to Shirley Schwaller 1946-2007

TWO DOGS HOWLING AT THE MOON: For my lifetime friend, Rusty Wier, a Hall of Fame songwriter with a double platinum song, "Don't It Make You Want To Dance," that was included in the sound track of the movie, *Urban Cowboy*.

SOMETIMES THE DARKNESS: Dedicated to Curtis Coleman. The lines "Sometimes the road leads through dark places. Sometimes the darkness is your friend," comes from, "Pacing the Cage," by Bruce Cockburn.

KNOWING TEXAS (2012): Portions of the poem were previously published in *The World Keeps Moving to Light: State Poets Laureate of America Renga* (Negative Capability Press.)

ABOUT THE AUTHOR:

David M. Parsons, 2011 Texas State Poet Laureate, is a recipient of many honors, including an NEH Dante Fellowship to SUNY Geneseo, the French-American Legation Poetry Prize, and the Baskerville Publisher's Prize from TCU for an outstanding poem published in their literary journal, *descant*. He holds eight writing awards from Lone Star College System and was inducted into The Texas Institute of Letters in 2009.

Parsons grew up in Austin, graduating from Stephen F. Austin High School. After which, he joined the United States Marine Corps Reserve, where he served as a Squad Leader in a rifle company and later as a Recon-Scout Boat Team Leader. He attended The University of Texas and Texas State University, where he holds a BBA. After several years in business, advertising, teaching Marketing and coaching basketball and baseball at Bellaire High School,

Parsons received his MA from the University of Houston's Graduate Creative Writing Program. He teaches Creative Writing and Racquetball/Handball at Lone Star College-Montgomery. Parsons has four grown children and lives with wife Nancy, an award winning Artist and Graphic Designer in Conroe, Texas. www.daveparsonspoetry.com

Books by David M. Parsons:

Editing Sky
Color of Mourning
Feathering Deep
David M. Parsons New & Selected Poems